PRAISE
MEETING HE

"This book is a walk down memory lane, but more important, an accurate depiction of the rise and evolution of women's athletics. As a high school coach for twenty-three years and a college coach for eleven, I have witnessed the days when opportunities for females were slim to none, to today when incredible experiences abound for all athletes. I loved each chapter of *Meeting Her Match*, and enjoyed the personal accounts of Debbie Millbern Powers's remarkable encounters. Thanks to Debbie for sharing her journey."
Dave Shondell, Head Women's Volleyball Coach, Purdue University

"Debbie Millbern Powers has accurately captured the essence of the times with insight into the challenges female athletes faced before the passage of Title IX. She brilliantly articulates the genuine joy we felt while playing sports. This book made me feel like I was on her team, experiencing every ounce of passion with each bounce of the leather ball."
Cheryl Feeney, Athletic Director & Former College Athlete

"It is said that nothing important in life ever comes easy. This book is a testimony to how true that really is. *Meeting Her Match* is clearly one of the best female sports stories ever told."
Steve Shondell, Head Women's Volleyball Coach, Ball State University

"Coach Millbern's memoir really hits the mark! It's not ever day that one gets to read a book about her own memorable past! As one of Coach Millbern's high school athletes, it was a joy to read her story and learn what was going on "behind the scenes." Coach Millbern was my role model on the court and in life."
Tricia Liston Kitchell, Physical Educator & Former High School Volleyball Player

"Little did our high school volleyball team know that we were about to encounter one of the largest challenges of our young lives ... and HE was 6'3"! Through this memoir I relived the thrills and chills of what it took to be a champion both on and off the court."
Cindy Parker Nestel, Retired Teacher & Former High School Volleyball Player

"Debbie captured the era prior to Title IX flawlessly. Her ability to depict the essence of the conditions for a female athlete during that time is exceptional. While reading her story, I was immediately transported back to my own experiences as a female athlete. *Meeting Her Match* is a must read for all female athletes for them to appreciate and understand the evolution of women's sports."
Renee' Turpa, Assistant Director, Indiana Basketball Coaches Association & Board Member, National High School Basketball Coaches Association

MEETING HER MATCH

The Story of a Female Athlete-Coach, Before and After Title IX

For Karen, my friend —
You are an inspiration to all women.
... for fitness & health.
I hope you enjoy Meeting Her Match!
Debbie

Debbie Millbern Powers

Meeting Her Match
Copyright © 2014 by Debbie Millbern Powers

Leeper Publishing
113 Village Las Palmas
St. Augustine, Florida 32080
USA

Cover design by Brenna Knotts
Cover art by Nathan Lewis
Photographs prepared by Perry Knotts

ISBN-13: 978-1495403187
ISBN-10: 1495403181

Library of Congress Control Number: 2014902879

Printed in the United States of America

A portion of the proceeds

from this book will be donated to

girls inc. ®

Inspiring all girls
to be strong,
smart, and bold[SM]

DEDICATION

This book is dedicated to the members of the Muncie Northside High School 1974 and 1975 girls' volleyball state championship teams. Your determination, courage, and spirit were an inspiration. You respected and cared about the sport....and felt the same way about each other. Furthermore, you successfully initiated and launched a young coach into a thirty-three year career that provided extraordinary fulfillment and joy. You were my first teams, and provided thrills and memories that have lasted a lifetime. I salute you champions in sport and life: Elizabeth Albright, Jane Amlin, Barb Cass, Cindy DeWitt, Debbie DeWitt, Joni Ewing, Carole Hagen, Perri Hankins, Polly Hankins, Tricia Liston, Sandy Lounsbury, Melissa Meredith, Cindy Parker, Sandy Schneiter, Christy Wagner, Shelley Walker, and Perri Williams.

AUTHOR'S NOTE

This is a true story. I have changed the names of many but not all of the individuals in this book, and, in some cases I also modified identifying details in order to preserve anonymity.

CONTENTS

FOREWARD by Bob Hammel

FOREWARD
by Bob Hammel – Former Newspaper Sports Editor

As I sat through the marvelous 2013 movie *42*, about Jackie Robinson's breakthrough into major league baseball, I thought of how young minds must have looked at Jackie's ordeal: *"Huh? Human beings treated other human beings like that? So recently?"* Can it be any different for young Americans who these days hear Title IX exalted? *"Huh, they needed a law to let girls compete in sports?"*

Yes, they—we—did. Stop and think about that a minute. How many laws passed in America's last 50 years have had as profound effect as Title IX, shorthand for the 1972 Equal Opportunity in Education Act? The law was intended to give girls the same opportunities as boys to develop their talents in medicine, law, engineering, and, as it turned out, athletics. We went, in just a few years, from medical school classes almost 90 percent male to 50 percent, with a similar effect in law and other prominent, well-paying professions. I think of my mother---how many like her, highly intelligent, consigned by home economics-not-science school curriculums to housewife lives when they might have been doctors *and* mothers. I think of my sister---the Debbie Millbern of our neighborhood---the best athlete on the block, but no team or uniform in her scholastic future.

Yes, kids, the America of "The Greatest Generation" and even a little beyond really did need laws to be even minimally humane in matters of race, creed, sexual preference, education…and sports. It was so easy to use *"That's the way it has always been"* to perpetuate rather than really look at issues that cried out for common-sense correction.

The best witnesses and story-tellers are people who lived on both sides of a profound change, and the very best are those who were victimized before unshackled. Maybe somebody like that has told this particular kind of story well. I have not seen it, not anything on this topic written so beautifully, so painfully, and so descriptively. Here, Debbie Millbern Powers---gifted athlete before Title IX's full effects, championship coach afterward---makes the injustices, triumphs, frustrations, and breakthroughs more than just believable. They are *feel*-able!

I was the university-town sports editor who gave her Indiana University basketball team minimal coverage, to the point where her and her team's best coverage in our newspaper came not in *Sports* but in a section of the paper called *Women*. Yeah, kids, really…in the 20th century! We all learned.

Here, Debbie lets us feel how one of the last victims of pre-Title IX discrimination felt, and we walk with her as one of the first to benefit, ever so gradually and slowly, court ruling by court ruling, toward true fairness in its classrooms, the professions, *and* the arena of sport.

Prepare to cry … in triumph.

PROLOGUE

NOVEMBER 15, 1975

The brakes on the big yellow school bus squealed as it rumbled to the curb. This ordinary, nondescript vehicle was about to deliver us to our destination of either triumph or defeat. Unlike the hundreds of other yellow school buses in the region, this one was far from ordinary. It was to be our chariot to battle, and hopefully greatness. Its accordion-like door opened slowly with a hissing sound and I watched my volleyball team move to ascend its giant steps. These eleven high school girls were in for the challenge of their young lives. Tonight's state championship match would be like no other. Regardless of who won, this match would go down in history, not just in our state, but across the country. It would be a topic of sports conversation for years to come. The circumstances of these finals would most likely never happen again. In fact, it should *never* happen again. As I watched the chattering teenagers, I had an overwhelming feeling of pride. What a group of fighters these kids were. I saw so much of me in them.

I pulled my coat tighter around my neck as I felt a sudden rush of cold from the early evening air. November in Indiana brought the first consistent wave of cold temperatures and, as a testament to that fact, a cloud of white vapor drifted into the air from the bus exhaust.

George, our bus driver, stepped out of the bus and approached me as I stood shivering on the sidewalk. He pulled a pair of gloves from his coat pocket and tugged them onto his hands. George was in his late fifties, a burly man with large, hairy arms, bushy eyebrows, and jowls that jiggled when he talked. George had driven our team to most of our out-of-town matches this season. Rather than staying on the bus during the competitions, he would sit by himself in the visitors' bleachers and cheer for us. He knew all the girls by name and cheered for them as if he had eleven daughters playing.

"Brrrrr." His voice quivered as he spoke. "Where'd this weather come from?"

I knew he didn't expect me to answer. Knowing George, he was trying his best to distract me from my preoccupation about the approaching match, or at least exude an air of normalcy and calmness to the moment.

"I'm just waiting for Susie. She went back for the athletic training kit," I said.

George stood silent as he looked back at the bus. We could hear the laughter of the girls over the soft rumbling of the engine.

"Are you ready for this, Coach?" he asked. His facial expression showed a mixture of inquisitiveness and panic.

"I've never been more ready," I replied without hesitation.

George shook his head slowly side to side. "You know, I still don't think this whole situation is fair."

"I know. Neither do I," I whispered back to him.

George placed his hand on my shoulder and gave me a gentle squeeze. "Tonight you'll make history, Coach Millbern."

CHAPTER 1

IN LOVE WITH BASKETBALL

I dove for the basketball as it was heading out of bounds. The stinging pain of gravel penetrated my elbow and knee causing me to grimace. My hand touched the rough leather-bound sphere just in time to flick it back onto the court. Still lying on the ground I felt a congratulatory slap on my back.

"Great save, Debbie," Billy shouted, as he punched me.

Billy was eleven, a year older than me, and my best friend in our neighborhood. A grin spread across my face as I picked myself off the ground and wiped the sweat off my forehead with my grimy hands. I glanced down at the bright red blood dripping down my leg onto my white sock. *Uh oh,* I thought, *Mom'll be mad.* She shouldn't be too surprised, though, since my knees were constantly covered with scabs. She'll probably just sigh and shake her head like she always does when she gathers my bloody, sweat-stained clothes for the laundry. My earliest memories as a young child were running and playing with balls. I loved to kick balls, throw balls, and catch balls. I was in constant motion, so by now Mom knew how rough I was on clothes.

With little hesitation I sprinted hard toward the basket with my hand raised to signal that I was open. Freckle-faced Paul bounced a pass to me behind my older brother Mike, and I laid the ball up against the backboard for an easy two points. Oh, how I loved to play basketball. I loved everything about it---the swishing sound as the ball sailed through the net, the clank of the rim when the ball hit it, the feel of the ball's rough texture on my fingers, and the sensation of flying through the air when I shot. To me the game was both magical and beautiful. I exulted in the pure physicality of it. I even liked the sweat and blood. Both were badges of effort.

It was 1961 and I lived in Indiana where the sport of basketball was a religion. In Muncie, the town in which we lived, the high school boys' basketball team had won more state championships than any other school in the state. Every Friday night during the cold winter months it seemed like the entire town was packed into the gymnasium. The Muncie Central Bearcats were local heroes.

I loved to go to the games with my dad. The hard-packed snow crunched under our boots as we hurried from the parking lot toward the warm gymnasium. I could see my breath in the air as I ran to keep pace with my dad and brother. The delicious aroma of buttery popcorn teased my nostrils when we entered the gym. Dad would hold my hand as we climbed to the top of the crowded bleachers. I would sit sandwiched between sweaty old men who smelled like cigarettes and beer. We were up so high that I could touch the rafters if I stood on my tip-toes. The adults around me would yell and scream at the referees and players, but I liked to quietly watch the game. I would study what the players on the court were doing and concentrated on one player at a time, memorizing his moves to replicate later in my own driveway. *Head fake; pull the ball back from the defender; jab step with the right foot; crossover step and drive hard to the basket.* Oh how I wanted to be that player, the one for whom everyone in the gym was cheering. Closing my eyes, I pretended the loud roars from the crowd were for me.

Like many houses in the Hoosier state, we had a basketball goal in our driveway. Ours was attached to the roof above the garage. I had begged Dad to put it up for me when we moved there. He complied I think only because he felt guilty about making me leave my friends and move to a new town the previous year. He understood how playing basketball brought me infinite joy. I would spend hours on that driveway court, in snow, rain, ice and scorching heat. All alone I would practice dribbling and shooting. Sometimes I would even voice a radio commentary as I played by myself: *"Millbern has the ball....she dribbles to her right....five seconds left....tie score....she jumps....shoots....it's goooooood!"*

I knew every crack and crevice in our concrete driveway, and because of the cycles of freezing and thawing, I would often have to sweep the loose gravel off various patches of the driveway before I played. Then, using a tape measure, I would meticulously measure fifteen feet from the basket and mark a free throw line with chalk. Sometimes I would challenge myself to see how many free throws I could make in a row. My record was 24, but I was determined to make 40 by the time I was twelve. Just like the players on television, I would go through the same routine before each free throw---place my right toe behind the line, bend my knees, bounce the ball three times, position my fingers on the seams, eye the basket, and launch the ball with a high arc and a flick of my wrist. It was almost intoxicating as I practiced shots from every spot, trying to sink more than I had the last time from that very spot....or make shots *without* the ball even touching the rim. Repetition and precision were the heart and soul of my drills.

From packed gymnasiums to playground courts, basketball was a social conduit in Indiana. At the weekly high school games men would talk politics while their wives gossiped. High school students would flirt while younger kids frolicked in the aisles. Playground courts were where friendships were made and petty conflicts resolved. Our driveway was a magnet for after-school basketball games. The neighborhood boys knew they could always find a game on our court.

This was one of those days. I hurried home from school, tore off my skirt and blouse, and slipped into purple cotton shorts and my older brother's cast-off gray T-shirt. *Ahhh, comfort*! I laced up my Keds, grabbed my basketball, and raced toward the front door, sidestepping my two little brothers, Tim and David, who had crayons scattered around the living room. They were drawing clowns and animals on white construction paper. Music from *American Bandstand* was blasting from our small black and white television.

Mom shouted from the laundry room, "Slow down, Debbie, and don't slam the door. Don't you have any homework?"

Her last sentence faded as I dashed out the door. Like a bird taking flight, I felt free. I began dribbling the ball up and down the driveway. I pivoted, faked and shot from various spots, racing toward the basket after every shot to rebound the ball. Soon I heard shouts from neighborhood boys riding their bikes toward our house. My brother Mike strolled out of the house and I could tell that he was contemplating whether to join in the game. He always tried to be cool and non-committal. I figured that he wanted to see who else would show up before he decided to honor us with his presence. Mike had jet-black hair just like our dad, and a sizable gap between his front two teeth. He was twelve, skinny, and a foot taller than me. Mike was constantly teasing me. His taunts were his method of keeping me in my place. He would continually inform me that I was inferior because I was two years younger, a girl, and not as smart as he was. My only edge over him was on the basketball court. I could outshoot him from any spot.

"Hey, Mike, come and play so we have an even number," I shouted as I dribbled the ball back and forth in front of me. The other boys nodded their heads to encourage him.

"Come on, Mike. We'll make sure that you don't have to guard your sister," Billy said with a snicker.

"Funny," Mike responded, making a contorted face at me. He hesitated for a moment as if he wanted us to continue to beg him. He lunged and grabbed the ball from me and shot a lay up. "Okay, I'll play," he said.

We picked sides and the battle began. Every one of these pick-up games was like a state championship. I played hard and never let up. I loved to compete and loved beating the boys. The chatter of basketball filled the air for the next two hours.

"Pick left!"

"Switch!"

"Nice shot."

"That's a foul!"

"Debbie, I'm open," Billy shouted. I dribbled to my left and executed a quick cross-over dribble. Striding out to my right I threw a perfect overhead pass to Billy. He jumped to shoot. I rushed past my defender toward the basket in anticipation of a rebound. Billy's shot bounced off the rim directly into my outstretched hands. I put it up and in for an easy two points.

"Debbbieeee!" My mom swung the front screen door open and appeared on the stoop, calling my name. Ignoring her, I crouched down to play defense.

"Debbie, come in and set the table for dinner," she shouted. I acted like I didn't hear her as I shuffled my feet while guarding Mike.

"Debbie!" I heard my name even louder, "I could use your help."

The game stopped. "Aw, Mom, do I have to?" I pleaded, even though I knew what her answer would be. Begging for equity I asked, "Doesn't Mike have to come in, too?"

"No. He's a boy and you're a girl. You need to help me in the kitchen," she answered.

Her words burned in my gut like a lightning bolt. "Because I'm a *girl*," I mumbled under my breath. "What does that have to do with it?"

Saying nothing, all of the boys glanced at me and then stared nervously at the ground. Mike laughed as he held the basketball on his hip.

"It's not fair," I shouted as I grabbed the ball from Mike and slammed it to the ground.

Mom retreated into the house and I followed slowly, wiping my sweaty face and newly-formed tears with my sleeve. I looked back at the boys as they fought each other for the ball and started playing again.

"No fair," I whispered again to myself as I defiantly stomped toward the bathroom to wash my hands.

"Use plenty of soap and hang up the towel," I heard Mom shout from the kitchen. I washed my hands and stared at my grimy face in the mirror.

"Boys are so lucky," I said to my reflection. I wiped my face and bloody knee with a towel and threw it to the floor.

At dinner the conversation revolved around Mike's school basketball games that were starting in a few weeks. I looked across the table at Mike.

"Aren't you excited about your first game?" I asked him.

He shrugged his shoulders and replied nonchalantly, "I guess so."

"I wish I could be on the team," I said. No one responded to my comment.

Mike and I attended the same elementary school, but he was two grades ahead of me. Three of my fourth-grade classmates were on the team with him.

"Your team should be pretty good this year," Dad said, as he reached for the bowl of mashed potatoes.

Dad had been a celebrated high school basketball player in the early 1940s. Growing up in the tiny town of Bourbon, Indiana, he was awarded a basketball scholarship to Ball State University, but World War II broke out and he enlisted in the Navy. After the war he married Mom and enrolled in embalmer's school. After earning his certification, he worked in the funeral business for awhile, eventually switching to the furniture business. It was common at one time for furniture manufacturers to also build caskets, so many funeral homes and furniture stores were connected. After Mike and I were born, Dad began spending more time in the furniture business, and now was the sole manager of a large local furniture store. Dad was full of personality and a terrific salesman. He was popular with customers because he always had a joke to tell. He had beautiful blue eyes and thick, black hair. I often wondered why he had initially chosen the funeral business because standing around at funeral services day after day didn't seem to fit his jovial personality. Dad seemed to enjoy being in the furniture industry, however, and worked long hours to support our family of six.

I loved it when Dad would come home after work and take the time to shoot baskets with me. I laughed when he first showed me how he used to shoot free throws in high school using a two-handed underhand motion. He would place both hands on the sides of the ball, squat down, and swing the ball up from between his legs. With perfect backspin the ball would swish cleanly through the net. This technique was far different from the free throw shooting method I observed in current players. I didn't laugh at his form very long, however, because he rarely missed. He had a beautiful overhead set shot too. As we played together he would teach me the fundamentals of the game. From my dad I inherited not only his striking blue eyes, but his love of basketball.

"Square your shoulders to the basket, Debbie. Keep your elbow under the ball. Flick your wrist when you follow through. Practice dribbling with your left hand just as much as you practice with your right hand. Follow your shot to the basket." I liked to pretend that he was my coach. My impression was that Dad was disappointed that Mike wasn't as passionate about the game as I was.

One evening Dad pulled into the driveway after work while I was shooting baskets. As a habit he parked the car at the very end of our narrow driveway to allow me plenty of space to play. In fact, the hood of his car had numerous indentations from stray passes that had missed their targets, but he never seemed to mind. It was past sunset and the fireflies were popping up like miniature light bulbs flickering in the warm evening air. The hum of cicadas resonated from a clump of trees across the street. I was winning championships in the dim glimmer of the street light, and the chirping of crickets was my only applause. Knowing that dinner would be served as soon as Dad arrived home, I had already sliced the carrots and tomatoes for the salad and escaped from the kitchen for a few more minutes of play outside.

"Hi, Dad!" I yelled to him as he exited the driver's seat. He had a shoebox under his arm as he trudged in my direction. Dad worked a long day, and it was evident by his slow step that he was tired.

"I've got something for you, honey," he said. He handed me the shoebox. I took off the lid and uncovered a pair of high-top Chuck Taylor All-Star basketball sneakers. They were white canvas with pearly white cotton shoestrings. I recognized these as the shoes the high school players wore.

"I hope they fit you. I had to guess the size, since they only come in boys' sizes."

My eyes were as wide as saucers as I stared into the box. I ran my fingers over the rough grooves in the brown rubber soles. I lifted the box to my nostrils. The rubbery smell reminded me of the Firestone Tire Store.

"But it's not my birthday or Christmas," I exclaimed.

"I know. I just thought you could use them," he replied. "Go ahead. Take them inside and try them on." His blue eyes glowed with excitement.

I gave him a long hug and then grabbed his hand. Ever since I was a small child, Dad and I had a secret hand squeeze. Whenever we were holding hands, either he or I would spontaneously squeeze three times: *I...love...you.* The other one of us would reciprocate with four squeezes: *I...love...you...too.* It was one of those small gestures that made me feel safe and loved. Tonight I initiated our silent hand squeeze message and he leaned down to kiss me on the head as he squeezed back.

I ran into the house with my treasure. Behind my closed bedroom door I slipped into the sneakers. They fit perfectly. I jumped around the room shooting imaginary jump shots. I felt like Cinderella in her magic slippers. The difference was that *my* Prince Charming was Dad, and he seemed fine in acknowledging that his only little girl was far from being a princess.

That evening Dad and I sat on the sofa watching a professional basketball game on television. I was wearing my pajamas along with my new Chuck Taylors. Mom was reading her *Ladies' Home Journal* while Mike was studying blades of grass with his Mr. Wizard microscope. My little brothers were already in bed. I loved to watch basketball games on TV. I knew everything about Oscar Robertson, Jerry Lucas, and Bob Cousy. During a break in the action I asked Dad why I never saw any girls playing on basketball teams. He responded that he didn't know why.

"I'll be good enough to play on TV someday," I announced. Dad chuckled and squeezed my leg with his hand. "In fact, I'm going to be a professional basketball player when I grow up and play in Madison Square Garden." Dad smiled and placed his arm around my shoulders and pulled me close to him. Mom looked up from her magazine, laughed, and winked at Dad. I didn't know what was so funny.

Mom tried her hardest to make me a "girlie" girl.
(with big brother, Mike)

Despite Mom's efforts,
I preferred to wear jeans, T-shirts, and sneakers!

CHAPTER 2

PLAYING WITH THE BOYS

I liked elementary school for two reasons: gym class and recess. I kept an old pair of corduroy slacks in my desk to put on under my skirt before going outside for recess. I played hard at recess and didn't want to feel restricted by having to wear a skirt. The girls in my class played hopscotch, jump rope, and four-square. I played basketball, baseball, and football with the boys. Those thirty minutes of recess everyday were heaven. I adored our gym teacher, Mr. Barnes. He was tall and muscular and had a crew-cut that was perfectly flat. A faint scent of after-shave filled the air whenever he walked by. I thought he was lucky to get to wear gym shoes and shorts everyday to school. Mr. Barnes often kidded me because I was always one of the first to be picked for teams by both the boys and the girls in my class. He called me his "little athlete" and I was proud to be considered the best athlete in the class. Several of the girls told me that they thought it was cool that I was so good at sports and the boys accepted me as one of their teammates. Some people, mostly adults, called me a "tomboy." I didn't like being called that because I didn't see how enjoying sports was exclusively linked to a word with "boy" in it. I saw myself as a *girl* who loved to play sports.

When Mr. Barnes had announced in our fourth grade gym class that he would be conducting tryouts for the school's basketball team, I had felt a rush of excitement. His announcement included proclamations about how much fun it would be to play on a team, how good character would be developed, and how skills for life would be learned. After class I rushed over to ask him if I could try out for the team. He patted me on the shoulder and told me that the team was for boys only.

Shocked and angry, I blurted out, "But can't girls have fun, develop character, and learn life skills, too?"

He shrugged his shoulders and said, "I'm sorry, Debbie, boys only." He turned to walk away and then hesitated. "You could always be a cheerleader, you know."

His words went through me like shrapnel. "A cheerleader!" I had shouted back at him. "That's boring! It's not fair because I'm better at basketball than any boy in this school."

Tears began to flood my eyes. I sat down on the gym floor and sobbed as the feelings of injustice and desperation engulfed me.

*****

One day the boys in my class and I were playing a lively game of flag football during recess. We wore shreds of old T-shirts in our waistbands as flags to tear off rather than tackling. We still ended up on the ground a lot. A shrill whistle from our teacher ended the game and we ran toward the building to line up. As we approached the building, my classmate Thomas teasingly grabbed a candy bar from Valerie. Valerie was a whiny, petite girl who always had an oversized bow attached to the back of her long brown hair. She was the spelling bee champion in our class so we kiddingly called her "bee-ny wee-ney" behind her back.

Valerie screamed when Thomas began tossing the candy bar among the boys in our class. Thomas tossed it to me and I tossed it to Andy. The other girls stood and watched as the boys and I played this keep-away game. As our teacher, Mrs. Edelman approached us, Thomas quickly handed the candy bar back to Valerie. Valerie immediately ran to Mrs. Edelman to tattle. As we stood quietly in our lines, Valerie proceeded to name everyone who had participated in the keep-away game. Of course that included me.

Mrs. Edelman was a tall, stately-looking woman who wore stylish dresses and high heels. She had perfectly-combed brown hair that flipped up at the ends and wore bright red lipstick. Her skin was smooth and creamy. If she wasn't a teacher, I concluded that she could have been a movie star. I didn't like her perfume, though. It made my nose itch. She ushered all of the girls into the classroom, sent the boys to the principal's office, and told me to stand alone in the hallway and wait for her. My legs shook and I could feel my heart beating against my chest as I leaned against the shiny brick wall. I looked down at my scuffed shoes and grass-stained slacks as I awaited my fate for participating in the keep-away game. Members of the sixth-grade class walked past me on their way to art class. Several of them pointed to me and giggled. I stuck my tongue out at them and was seized by a feeling of dread: *Mom is going to kill me when she finds out I got in trouble.*

Mrs. Edelman came out of the classroom and closed the door behind her. "Debbie, look at me," she said. I looked up at her and tried not to cry. She was not smiling, and her eyes looked like they could pierce my skin. With a harsh tone she said, "You need to stop playing with the boys so much and act more like a girl."

I stared at her as tears filled my eyes and I thought to myself, *Act more like a girl? What does she mean by that? I am a girl. I'm a girl who happens to like playing sports.*

I remained silent as Mrs. Edelman continued. "It's not normal for girls to play as aggressively and competitively as you do. You need to spend your recess playing with the other girls in the class. If you like sports, I suggest you try cheerleading."

I blinked back my tears and choked out a feeble response. "Yes, ma'am, I guess so."

Mrs. Edelman shook her finger at me. "And besides, if you win all of the time, no one wants to play with you---especially if you're a girl!"

Her final statement drove a stake into my heart: *especially if you're a girl.* Her face suddenly transformed into a witch's, and I felt a weakening in my knees---the kind of weakening I'd feel if someone told me that my mom or dad had been hurt in an accident. I took a few deep breaths to maintain my composure. Mrs. Edelman had spoken her last sentence with such conviction that I couldn't muster the courage to respond. I was suffering from an acute case of confusion.   I didn't understand what she meant, because whenever I faced a competitor who was a consistent winner, it made me try *harder*.   I certainly didn't hate them and I'd never consider quitting--- whether it was against a girl *or* a boy!

As she motioned for me to go back into the classroom I felt a mixture of emotions. Feelings of anger, frustration, and embarrassment gripped me. Her harsh words echoed in my ears: *not normal...shouldn't be aggressive...play with the other girls...try cheerleading...no one likes a girl who wins.* I sat at my desk, staring out the window and tried to make sense of her words. Why am I different from the other girls? I don't like dolls.   I don't care about fashion.   Girls' games are boring to me. Yet, the girls still like me as their friend. And cheerleading? Both Mr. Barnes and Mrs. Edelman had suggested I be a cheerleader. It disgusted me to watch cheerleaders jumping around cheering for the boys. Most of the time they didn't even know what was happening in the games. I hated cheerleading!

The next day at recess we organized a game of kickball on the black asphalt playground. The asphalt had white painted boxes designating the bases. I was relieved when a couple girls decided to play, so I felt comfortable joining in too. My guess was that Mrs. Edelman wouldn't object since it was girls and boys playing together. During one particular play I was on second base and my teammate Andy kicked a long ball. I sprinted around third and headed for home plate. Knowing that it would be a close play, I slid on the asphalt across home plate as the ball missed hitting me and soared over my head. As I reveled in the cheers from my teammates, I stood up and felt searing pain on my upper thigh. I lifted my skirt and saw bloody flesh through the torn threads of my corduroys. I winced as I lightly touched my thigh. Obviously I was now paying the price for sliding on asphalt, but the competitiveness of the moment had overtaken me. Since recess was almost over, I hurried toward Mrs. Edelman, who was sitting on a bench talking with two other teachers. I walked as normally as possible, even though my thigh was screaming at me. Thankfully my skirt covered the gaping holes in my slacks. I politely asked permission to go to the bathroom. She said "okay," but told me to hurry since recess was almost over.

Once inside the bathroom I stripped off my slacks and examined my upper thigh. It was a large scrape that was bloody and oozing. I grabbed some paper towels, soaked them with soap and cool water and applied them to my wound. The relief from the burning was only temporary as I pulled the compress off and reapplied another. The bell ending recess blasted through the building and I could hear the footsteps of my classmates outside the bathroom door heading toward our classroom. In a panic I carefully applied a fresh paper towel compress and pulled a long strip of material off my torn slacks. It was my only means of securing the compress to my thigh. I thought about using a long strand of toilet paper, but, unlike home, the school toilet paper was individual squares. Having individual squares always seemed so wasteful to me and the other girls as we pulled multiple squares from the metal holder to use, and then left just as many lying on the floor as they tumbled out of the holder. I wrapped my thigh the best I could, threw what remained of my torn slacks into the trash can, and limped carefully back to class.

Several times during the rest of the day I discreetly lifted my skirt to check my wound. I knew that I should probably go to see the school nurse, but I was afraid of what Mrs. Edelman would say. One admonishment from her about my competitiveness had been enough.

Once home I sprayed Bactine on my scrape, biting on a towel to muffle my gasps of pain from the stinging antiseptic. I continued to clean and dress my wound with gauze for several days until it healed, successfully hiding my injury from Mom. I vowed that I'd never slide on the asphalt again (unless perhaps it was a tie-breaking score).

*****

On the day of Mike's first basketball game I hurried to the gym and sat in the bleachers, waiting for my mom and dad to arrive. Our team was wearing shiny blue shorts and yellow jerseys with huge blue numbers on the backs. The boys on the team who were in my class waved to me as they took their warm-up shots.

"Good luck," I shouted to them as I waved back to them. I waved to my brother Mike, but he ignored me. The enticing aroma of popcorn drifted in from the hallway where the sixth-graders sold popcorn and candy to earn money for their end of the year class trip.

Mom arrived with my two little brothers in tow. Dad came after the game had already started, still wearing his suit and tie. The game was a calamity. The referees blew their whistles every twenty seconds as double-dribbles, missed passes that sailed out of bounds, and tie-ups dominated the game. Missed shots ricocheted off the backboard. I shouted instructions to the boys.

"Andy, take him to his left," I yelled. "Spread the floor. Follow your shots. Box out for the rebound!" These were basketball fundamentals that seemed natural to me, having internalized them during hours of practice. I shifted my weight back and forth as I sat on the bleachers as if my body was playing the game.

I looked at Mr. Barnes. He was sitting quietly on the bench watching the game as if he was a mere spectator rather than their coach. *Why hasn't he taught these boys the fundamentals?* I thought. *Why isn't he shouting instructions?*

Dad shouted at Mike, and Mom tried to keep my little brothers occupied. We lost the game, 26-19. As we were leaving the gym, Andy walked over and grabbed my arm.

"We would have won if you were on the team, Debbie," he said. "You're better than anyone out here."

I felt a sudden glow of pride, then an overwhelming surge of sadness as I trailed my family outside into the December chill. "It's not fair that I can't play on that team," I mumbled as I pulled my stocking cap down over my ears.

That night Mom came into my room to hear my prayers. She sat down and stroked my hair as I knelt beside my bed. My night-time prayer was a memorized mantra that I repeated nightly: *Now I lay me down to sleep. I pray thee Lord, my soul to keep. If I should die before I wake. I pray thee Lord, my soul to take. Amen.* I often wondered why a ten-year-old girl should be worried about dying before she awakened, but I never questioned it.

I jumped into bed and Mom tucked me in and gave me a good-night kiss. Dad was doing the same ritual with my brothers, and I presumed also talking to Mike about his performance in the game. Once Mom had left my room I stared at the ceiling. A small streak of light from the street lamp slipped in between the yellow, polka dot curtains. A faint hint of lavender filled my nostrils from my freshly laundered flannel pajamas and sheets. I felt safe as I heard the muffled sounds of my parents talking in the living room.

During the stillness of the night, however, my mind would not rest. My heart ached. More than anything in the world I wanted to play on a real basketball team. I wanted a coach like Mr. Barnes and a shiny uniform with numbers on the back. I wanted to play for my school. I wanted to be an athlete. I thought about what Mrs. Edelman had said to me in the hallway at school, and what Andy had told me after the game. Even Mr. Barnes's words *"boys only"* echoed inside my head. At school our teachers were constantly reminding us of how fortunate we were to live in America, a free country where men and women have choices. We were told that we could grow up to be anything we wanted to be. "Follow your dreams," our teachers said. We were told to find our passion and work hard to develop our talents. I was talented at sports, worked hard at sports, and had a passion for sports. So where was my future? I never saw girls playing sports on television or read about girls playing sports in the newspaper. I never read stories or saw pictures of girls playing sports in books. There were no female sportscasters, coaches, or referees. Most of the athletic girls became cheerleaders, but that didn't interest me at all. I wanted people cheering for *me*. A tear rolled down my cheek and fell onto my pillow.

I quietly pushed back my bed covers and dropped down to my knees on the hardwood floor beside my bed. I shivered as I felt the cool draft from under the bed. I folded my hands, bowed my head, and whispered my prayer: *"Dear God, I hope you're still there, because I forgot to tell you something tonight in my prayers. I have a huge favor to ask. You know how much I like to play sports. In fact you made me to be a good athlete. So,...*(I hesitated and took a deep breath) *could you please turn me into a boy during the night so I can play on a real team? I know it's a weird request, but I don't see any other way that I'll be able to do what I want to do. Thank you, God. Amen."*

I started to crawl back into bed but dropped down to my knees one more time: *"Oh, and by the way, God, I'm not ready to die if you're thinking about that for me tonight."*

I climbed into bed and snuggled under the soft covers to get warm. Wrapping my arms around my teddy bear that had a miniature basketball in its paws, I closed my eyes. Sleep started to come as feelings of contentment and hope embraced my heart.

With little brothers, Tim and David

CHAPTER 3

MOVING....AGAIN

"We're moving to a new town," Dad announced at dinner.

I dropped my fork and stared at him. Mike continued to shovel food into his mouth, and my younger brothers looked at me for a cue as to how to react.

"I've taken a new job, so your mother and I will be putting the house up for sale and searching for one in our new town," Dad continued.

Since I had heard this announcement several times in my life, I repeated my same complaints. "I don't want to move. I don't want to leave my friends. I hate being the new girl in school."

Like rote memorization from past conversations, Dad replied, "It'll be exciting, and you'll make a lot of new friends."

The misery of adjusting to a new school and new friends was a continuing saga in my young life. It was never fun, and it got harder with each move. And now, starting junior high school as a seventh-grader, I looked at it as social death. All of the towns in which we had lived were in Indiana---Plymouth, Bourbon, Bremen, Kokomo, and Muncie. Attending five different elementary schools had been painful. With every move I experienced a profound feeling of displacement. It took half the school year to finally feel comfortable and develop solid friendships. The ritual was always the same. The first students in the class who wanted to be your friend were the ones who no one else liked. They would latch onto new kids like leeches in a pond. It took awhile to sort through them to find potential friends. After I finally reached a level of comfort and happiness, Dad would make another change-of-job announcement and my new school and new friends would disappear again from my life. It would have been nice to have close friends for more than a year or two. Mom always told me that our multiple moves had helped me become independent and resilient. I viewed it as torture.

Dad was always looking for a better job, one that paid more money or provided better benefits. His jobs always revolved around the furniture business, either working in retail or traveling around a territory as a manufacturer's representative. Once he accepted a new job, he and Mom would travel to the new town for a weekend and find a house. It had to have four bedrooms: one for my parents, one for Mike, one to be shared by my little brothers, and one for me. Being the only girl at least gave me a single bedroom privilege.

Mom was a trooper through all of our moves. She would stay back with us kids at the current house until it sold, which meant we had to keep everything tidy and clean for spontaneous realtor showings. Everyday before we left for school all beds were neatly made, books and clothes picked up off the floor, dirty dishes washed, and furniture dusted. This got to be our ordinary before-school routine since our houses were periodically on the market. Mom had the brunt of the work, but we kids were expected to do our part. Dad would spend the weekdays at his new job and then come home for the weekend. Mom was also responsible for packing, unpacking, and decorating the new house. With four kids, there was a lot to pack. Mom would walk into our bedrooms, do a slow 360-degree pivot and announce that we were to get rid of half the stuff we owned before each move. Only the essentials could go with us. I would sort through my drawers and closet and toss out academic award certificates, books, trinkets, posters, hats, pictures, farewell cards, stuffed animals and T-shirts with my school's logo. Memories of that period of my life ended up in either the trash or in our garage sale. To her credit, Mom was a master at conducting garage sales, and she prided herself in the amount of money she would earn by selling our "junk" before each move.

Her responsibilities left us kids fending for ourselves a lot, which was fine with me. Since I was the only girl, however, I was expected to take care of my little brothers while Mom was busy with moving tasks. Mike never had to babysit. He insisted that his job was to be the "substitute dad" since our real dad was gone so much.

"That's not fair," I told Mike. "And besides, Dad never yanks my ponytail or punches me in the ribs like you do."

While Dad and Mom continued to chat over dinner about his latest job offer and our impending move, I asked to be excused from the table. They nodded their approval and I carried my dishes to the sink. I was frustrated and unhappy.

"This is so unfair," I interrupted their conversation. "Both of you got to go to the same school in the same town from kindergarten all the way through high school. You have no idea how hard it is to change schools so many times." My voice began cracking. "I don't know why you keep doing this to me."

My brothers stared at me, but said nothing. I stomped out of the kitchen, grabbed my basketball, and ran out to our driveway. With the street light and a dim yellow light bulb above our garage door, the basketball goal was only partially illuminated. There was a slight mist in the cool evening air that created a mystical glow. I frantically began shooting and dribbling. The reverberating sound of the ball pounding the pavement began numbing my pain. This was my haven. This was where I was happy and had total control. Playing basketball provided tranquility amid the chaos in my life.

An hour flew by and I retreated into the house. My clothes were damp with sweat. Tiny droplets had formed on my hair from the moisture in the air. I walked past my dad who was engrossed in the evening paper.

"All I can say is that our new house better have a basketball goal," I said to him defiantly. Not waiting for his answer I went into my room and slammed the door.

*****

My mother was pretty. She wore bright red lipstick and red polish on her fingernails and toenails. She had her hair done at a salon twice a month and never seemed to have a hair out of place, even when she got out of bed in the morning. She was slim and liked to dress in the latest fashions. Her shoes always matched her outfits, and the scent of her perfume lingered throughout the house.

Mom's monthly social outing was a bridge club where twelve ladies met to gossip and play cards. When she hosted the club, I volunteered to fill the candy dishes at each table. With that job I could sneak handfuls of mixed nuts and Brach's chocolates, appropriately called "bridge mix." I loved to linger in the doorway and watch the ladies play. Their chatter filled the room, accompanied by only the clicking sound of cards being shuffled and dealt. Most of the ladies smoked cigarettes creating a cloudy haze throughout the living room.

I could never understand why so many adults smoked. Both Mom and Dad smoked a lot, and so did their friends. While riding in the car we kids would beg Mom and Dad to open a window while they smoked. Otherwise my eyes would burn and I felt like I was choking. I told them our teachers taught us that smoking was bad for you. They agreed with our teachers, but acknowledged that they enjoyed smoking and were addicted. I pleaded with them to try to stop. They never did.

Mom was an excellent bridge player and would complain to us when she had been paired with an inferior player. Watching her intensity at the bridge table convinced me that I might have inherited some of my competitive nature from my mother as well as from my dad.

At Plymouth High School, Mom had been a cheerleader and the homecoming queen. Looking through her high school yearbook and reading her classmates' comments, I could tell that she had been one of the most popular girls in her school. She and Dad started dating when they were seventeen. He was the handsome all-star athlete and she was the all-American girl. They were only nineteen when they got married.

Occasionally in the evenings Dad would put on a record and he and Mom would jitterbug in the living room. We kids would gather on the sofa and clap as Dad swung Mom around. They'd twist their hips and kick their feet out, smiling and laughing I was amazed at their agility and how fluidly they moved. The sounds of Glenn Miller's *In the Mood* and the Andrews Sisters filled the house. We'd try to sing along....*"He's the boogie woogie bugle boy of Company B."* It was fun to see Mom and Dad giggling and dancing rather than just working all the time. Somehow neither of them dropped the cigarette that dangled from their lips. In my eyes they were the coolest parents around.

One summer day I came inside from playing to get a drink of water. Mom was smoking cigarettes and watching *As the World Turns* on television. She called the show "her story" and rarely missed it. Soap operas seemed boring to me, but I sat down and watched for a few minutes while I drank my water.

"Mom," I said, "I have a question for you."

"Wait until the commercial, Debbie," she replied.

I waited patiently until the break when an announcer sang a little jingle asking viewers if their clothes came out of the washing machine as clean as they liked. I pushed aside her pack of Pall Malls on the coffee table and set down my glass.

"Mom, did you ever play basketball?"

"Of course I did. I played intramurals when I was in college. And I was pretty good," she replied, taking another puff on her cigarette. I watched the smoke circle into the air when she exhaled. I remembered that Mom had told me once that she had attended a private women's college for one year, but quit when the war ended to marry Dad.

"But why did you stop playing?"

She laughed. "Because I got married and began having babies."

"Don't you miss playing?"

"Of course not. I have all of you kids to take care of. I get enough exercise running from the kitchen to the laundry room to the grocery store to the bedrooms to the living room...." She stopped talking because her story was coming on again.

I sat for a little while longer, thinking about what she had just said. I poked a finger into my glass and played with an ice cube. *If having babies and cleaning the house is what I have to look forward to when I grow up, I'll be miserable,* I thought.

I carried my glass back to the kitchen and headed out the door. I looked back through the screen and watched my mother sitting on the sofa as she lit another cigarette. Blaring from the television was the start of another show.

"How would YOU like to be QUEEN for a DAY?" I heard the host shouting.

Jeez, I thought to myself, *is that what being a grown up woman is about---wanting to be a queen, winning a refrigerator, and worrying about how clean the laundry is? Will the highlight of my life be collecting enough sheets of S & H green stamps to earn a free skillet or waffle iron?*

I chuckled as I jumped onto my bike and headed down the street. My smile soon faded to feelings of frustration and sadness. I wondered if Mom was disappointed that she never finished college. Did she regret not playing sports anymore? One thing for sure, she didn't need those things to be a good mother because she was devoted to us. I worried, though, that she might be disappointed that her only daughter was not a "girlie" girl who loved frilly dresses, tea parties, and shopping. Mom would merely shake her head and roll her eyes when I stormed into the house all sweaty with streaks of dirt on my face.

"Gotta go to the bathroom," I'd shout as I ran down the hall with my pants already half pulled down.

"Don't forget to wash your hands," she'd shout back to me.

The only time I remembered that she had loudly voiced her disapproval was the Christmas when my grandmother gave me a doll for a gift. I defiantly threw it down, telling my grandmother that I'd rather have a baseball glove. Mom was livid with me.

Most of the time I figured that Mom was so overwhelmed with her job as a wife and mother that she didn't have the time or energy to mold me into the ideal daughter. She had enrolled me in a ballet class one time. That was a disaster. I begged her not to make me go anymore after I made so many mistakes at the recital. I endured Brownies for a year until I got tired of weaving leather coin purses and planting flowers. Next was baton twirling class, at which I was pretty good, but I found to be extremely boring. I didn't see the point in tossing a small steel stick into the air while pirouetting below it. If Mom was disappointed in me, she didn't show it. As long as I did my chores and helped with my little brothers, she didn't seem to care what I did with my free time.

I wouldn't say that the forecast for my future was one of despair, but there was a sense of uncertainty and dread that lingered in my mind. The adult women with whom I was personally acquainted were mothers, teachers, secretaries, nurses, or bank tellers. I never saw a female lawyer, politician, architect, television reporter, or doctor, let alone an athlete. The majority of women I saw on television programs rarely left their kitchens. Even the women in *Leave It to Beaver*, *Ozzie and Harriet*, and *Father Knows Best,* my favorite weekly programs, wore dresses and aprons. They cooked, cleaned, and shopped. I never saw them participating in any sports, exercising, or even tossing around a ball with their kids in their front yards. The prepubescent girls on these programs were often crying and portrayed as helpless. In fact, these television images of adult women mirrored what I saw in my own world. Women were treated as if they were incapable of being a mechanic, engineer, or CEO. This confused me because Mom once told me that many women built airplanes during the war. Now, however, I saw women priding themselves in a good pot roast or spotless linoleum floor. My confusion was blossoming into serious aggravation as I felt the sting of being forced to sit on the sidelines and boost the egos of boy athletes.

One time during an airplane trip with my family, I decided it would be exciting to be an airline stewardess and travel all over the world. It seemed like a career that would feed my adventurous spirit. Then I learned that stewardesses were required to wear high heels, maintain a prescribed weight, and lost their jobs if they got married. And, they had to retire at age thirty-two! Those requirements nixed my desire to be a stewardess. In contrast, the male pilots I saw in the airport obviously didn't have the same restrictions as the stewardesses. Many of the pilots were plump and old. Most also wore wedding bands. I asked my mother why I didn't see any female pilots. I imagined that flying the airplane would be more fun than serving coffee to passengers.

"Why would a woman want to be a pilot?" Mom answered me.

*****

Pulling into our newest town, Dad drove past Conroy Junior High School so that I could see my new school. He did this before we arrived at our new house. I guess he wanted me to feel reassured that it was a normal-looking school. It looked normal enough to me, but I dreaded what I would face in a few weeks behind those red brick walls.

We could see the big yellow and green moving van parked in our driveway when we pulled into our subdivision. The first thing I noticed was that our house didn't have a basketball goal, but Dad promised to put one up as soon as we got settled. As I wandered from room to room in our new house, I heard Mom directing the men where each box should go. Since I was little help to anyone, I asked Mom for permission to walk around and check out the neighborhood. She agreed and told me to not stray too far.

All of the houses in the neighborhood looked alike, one-story ranch-style with gray roofs and brick fronts. The only variations were the garage doors. Some were painted white, others brown, some beige, and a few blue. Three doors down from our house was an empty lot where a bunch of boys were playing baseball. Since they looked close to my age, I felt a rush of excitement and quickened my pace.

"Hi," I shouted to the boys, as I stood at the curb.

"Is that your moving van?" a boy with blonde hair asked. His voice cracked a little when he spoke.

I nodded. "Yep, we just moved here."

Since no one else said anything to me, I stood and watched the game. Like many pick-up baseball games, the teams were lopsided. Each team had a pitcher and two infielders. One team had three outfielders while the other team had only two outfielders. The team at bat was providing the catcher.

"Mind if I play?" I asked.

Another boy who was getting ready to bat turned to me and answered, "I guess so. Go out in the outfield. That'll even the teams." He turned and grinned to his teammates and took a few practice swings.

I ran though the thick weeds and dandelions that littered the overgrown field to a position in right field. I bent over and placed my hands on my knees ready to move after each pitch. Grasshoppers kept popping up among the weeds and small sticky thistles were clinging to my socks. No balls were hit my way and my team headed to home plate to bat. Home plate was a jagged piece of cardboard.

"When do I bat?" I asked a small stocky boy with red hair. I had heard the boys call him Red.

"Last," the boys chimed together with a laugh.

"You gonna go to Conroy Junior High?" Red asked me.

"I guess so," I answered. "Is it a good school?"

"I guess so," Red answered as he swatted at a bee flying around his head.

When it was finally my turn to bat, I took a few practice swings and established a crouched stance at home plate. I noticed that the boys in the outfield had moved in close to the infield, anticipating a short hit. I had watched the pitcher the previous inning and noticed that his first pitch was pretty wild, so I let his first pitch go by me. True to form it was low and way outside my reach. The next pitch came right down the middle and I swung the bat across my body as fast as I could, watching the ball hit the solid part of the bat. The ball sailed high into the air, over all of the boys' heads and continued over the fence of the house next to the vacant lot. The loud sound of splintering glass filled the air. I stopped running around the bases when I heard the crash.

Everyone shouted in unison, "Oh no!"

"Great," I mumbled to myself. "My first day in a new town and I broke a neighbor's window."

We all ran toward the broken window to survey the damage. It looked like it was a bedroom window which was now shattered into thousands of pieces scattered among the shrubs and grass. My stomach was doing flip flops as I slowly walked around the house toward the front door. The boys followed me.

"They're probably at work," one of the boys said.

No one answered the door when I knocked, so I turned to walk toward my house thinking about facing my parents. *Maybe they should just kill me*, I thought. *Then I won't ever have to go to Conroy Junior High.*

As I began plodding toward my house I heard Red shout to me. "That was some hit. Wanna play tomorrow?"

"If I'm still alive," I answered with a grin on my face.

"Great! Be sure to get the baseball when you go back over to that house tonight. It's the only one we have."

As I expected Mom was livid that I broke our neighbor's window. Dad seemed somewhat amused by it. Mom slapped her hand on the kitchen counter. "Jeez, Debbie, our first day in the neighborhood! As soon as someone is home over there you will march over and apologize. And, you will pay for the window from your allowance!"

I sat on the front porch tossing a tennis ball in the air waiting for some sign of life at the neighbor's. A feeling of dread overwhelmed me once I saw a black Chrysler pull into their driveway. I waited a few minutes then walked across the street and knocked on the front door. I felt a knotting in my stomach when I heard footsteps from behind the door and a heavy deadbolt lock unlatching. Before me stood a tall balding man with wisps of bright red hair sticking out on the sides of his head above his ears. He looked like Bozo the Clown, except that he was wearing a brown herring-bone suit instead of a polka-dotted clown suit. He had deep-set blue eyes and pasty white skin. I could hear classical music playing in the background on a radio.

"Hi, I'm Debbie." I said, as I thrust my hand forward to shake his. "We just moved in across the street."

When he didn't extend his hand to me, I pulled mine back and stuck it deep into my pocket. I continued, speaking as fast as I could, hoping that my words would somehow evaporate into the air without him hearing them.

"This afternoon I was playing baseball with some boys in the lot next to your house and I hit a baseball over your fence and broke one of your windows. I am so sorry about it and I plan to pay for it. Will $5 a week work for you?" Out of breath, I paused while studying his reaction.

He placed his hands on his hips and stared at me, saying nothing for what seemed like an eternity. I felt like I was either going to throw up or pee right on his front step. Finally he spoke.

"Well, Debbie, I hadn't even noticed the window. I just got home from work." He spoke softly with no emotion of anger or excitement.

He disappeared into the house for a few moments and returned with the baseball in his hand.

"This must be yours," he said, as he cupped the ball in his hand. "That must have been quite a hit. Was it a fastball or a curve ball?"

Startled by his question, I hesitated, then answered. "It was a fastball right down the middle."

"Good for you," he replied. "You know what? My sister played professional baseball for the Springfield Sallies in the '40s. I don't know if she could have hit a ball that far when she was your age." He smiled and I felt a sudden wave of relief.

"Here's your ball back, and don't worry about the window."

I took the ball, thanked him, and ran back home, wondering who the Springfield Sallies were. I had never heard of girls playing professional baseball. *Hmm, maybe I could do that someday,* I thought.

Mom and Dad

CHAPTER 4

JUNIOR HIGH LESSONS

The first day in my new neighborhood had certainly been memorable, but my first day at Conroy Junior High School was traumatic. Even though the school held only seventh- and eighth-graders, it was bigger than any of my previous schools, and the transition to the new routine of changing classes, having lockers, and facing a variety of teachers every day was difficult enough without having to also be the *new* girl.

Junior high school was all about insecurity, pimples, and fitting in. Since all of the other kids had gone to elementary school together, I felt like an outcast. No longer would there be recess where I could display my athletic talents and find my niche. And, unlike elementary school, gym classes were segregated to be all girls or all boys.

As I maneuvered around the building that first morning trying to find my English classroom, then social studies and math classes, my stomach hurt and my hands remained sweaty. Some of the girls were wearing make up. Some wore bras. I wore neither. Some of the boys were tall and had deep voices. Some of the boys were shorter than me. A few boys and girls held hands as they walked down the hall. At lunchtime I sat by myself and surveyed the scene. It was easy to spot the "in crowd," as they talked, laughed, and pointed at other students. They wore freshly-pressed designer clothes. A couple of the girls wore cheerleading sweaters. Apparently the cheerleaders had been chosen at the end of the previous school year. The nerdy kids were all gathered around an open encyclopedia volume that one of them had brought to the lunchroom. Sitting all around the room and chatting were "best friends" from previous years. No one paid attention to me and I felt adrift among the snubs. I looked for the boys I had met playing baseball during the summer but didn't see any of them. The noise in the lunchroom was deafening with loud voices, scooting chairs, and clanging dishes merging into one large roar.

I looked down at my pale green plastic lunch tray. It had six divided sections—salisbury steak covered with a gelatinous dollop of gravy, peas swimming in a buttery pool, four partially-burned Tater Tots, half a peach, a sugar cookie, and a half-pint carton of milk. I concentrated on eating, since no one was sitting near me. Since I wanted enough time to find my next class, I ate quickly and hurried to return my tray to the huge black conveyer belt that was rumbling in the far corner of the lunchroom. The belt was littered with assorted plastic trays, milk cartons, stray Tater Tots, rolling peas, crumpled napkins, and scattered silverware. As I walked out of the lunchroom, I saw Red, the boy with whom I had played baseball over the summer. He waved and I smiled at him, happy to finally see a familiar face.

"Hi, Red," I said cheerfully.

"What's wrong with your eye?" he asked.

I immediately touched my right eye. I had noticed that it felt a little strange during lunch, but figured I had an eyelash in it.

"Why, what's wrong with it?" I asked.

"It's all red and weird-looking," he responded.

I ran down the hall to the closest girls' bathroom. Several girls were gathered around the sinks putting on lipstick and mascara and talking about their boyfriends. I leaned toward the closest mirror. The white part of my right eye was bright red, and I could tell that the upper eyelid was slightly swollen. I began splashing water onto my face and held water in my cupped hand directly on my eye as the other girls glanced over at me. I looked in the mirror again. No change. *Great. I look like a freak*, I thought.

A loud bell rang throughout the building to signal the next class period, so I scurried down the hall to my science classroom. I slid into a seat in the back corner, hoping that no one would look at me. As I listened to the monotone drone of the teacher going over the class rules, I could feel my right eye beginning to swell even more. My left eye was doing the same. My vision was becoming blurry as my eyelids continued to swell. I began to panic. *What am I going to do? Should I go up to the teacher? What will all the other kids say? I look like a monster. How embarrassing!*

Finally, the girl sitting at the desk beside me looked at me and shouted to the teacher. "Something's wrong with her eyes!"

Everyone in the class turned and stared at me. Though they appeared blurry to me, I could see their astonished expressions. Some snickered. I wanted to melt into the floor like the wicked witch in *The Wizard of Oz*. The teacher hurried toward me and gently took my arm to escort me from the room. We proceeded to the nurse's office, and she called my mother. Mom arrived quickly and guided me to our car as I began crying.

"I hate this school. I never want to go back! They'll think I'm a freak!" I sobbed.

"Oh, honey, no they won't. What the heck did you eat for lunch?" Mom asked as she drove me home.

Whether it was something I ate that day or simply nerves, a few doses of Benadryl took care of the problem. A few hours later, after school was out, there was a knock on our front door. I opened the door and there stood Red with a handful of papers.

"Here, Debbie, I brought your papers from the classes you had to miss today."

I thanked him, and Mom invited him in for some cookies.

"No, thank you. I'm heading over to the field to play baseball. Wanna come, Debbie?"

I looked longingly at Mom, but could read that her face was answering "No."

Red interpreted her answer, as well, and began running toward the vacant lot. He turned and shouted to me, "See you in school tomorrow."

I waved to him and knew I had at least one friend at Conroy Junior High School.

*****

Shortly after we were settled, Dad kept his promise and installed a basketball goal in our driveway. Our driveway became the preferred site for pick-up games in the neighborhood. Some of Mike's ninth-grade classmates would come and play. A few of his friends were even older and played on the high school team. They were tall and strong, but they always let me play, even though I was smaller. While playing against them I learned to shoot a jump shot. My upper body was finally strong enough for me to jump high into the air and loft a shot at the top of my jump. I had been watching guys shoot jump shots for several years, and was excited to finally be able to duplicate this technique. My new practice regimen was to shoot jump shots from various spots on the court. Even though my range was only eight feet from the basket, I knew it would extend as I got stronger.

Although I could not play one-on-one against these bigger boys, I could still compete against them in shooting contests. They were constantly challenging me to shooting games, and I could tell from their expressions that they felt a huge measure of accomplishment if they would win. I loved playing against the guys, and they were nice to me. I actually had a crush on one of the guys, but I still tried hard to beat him. Whereas most prepubescent girls would be giddy or timid in the midst of high school boys, I could not quiet the competitive urges housed in my soul.

With no organized girls' sports at my school, these driveway games meant everything to me.

Because there was no recess in junior high school, my only other athletic outlet was gym class. Most of the girls in my gym class complained about having to change into our assigned gym uniforms, sweating, showering, and messing up their hair and makeup. Many of the girls skipped the shower, not wanting to display their changing bodies to a crowd. There were girls in all stages of development, and this was the first time this realization hit many of us. We were all changing, but on different time clocks.

The girls' gym uniforms were ugly, but I was always glad to get out of my skirt for an hour each school day and play in the gym. Our white gym shorts had elastic around each leg that hit at mid-thigh, creating a ballooning effect around our butts and stomachs. The white shirts were stiff cotton with tight short sleeves. Our last names were printed in a box across our chests with black magic marker.

A heavy folding door separated the gym into two sections. The boys were on one side and the girls on the other. There was one other girl who was a pretty good athlete in my gym class, so we became fast friends. We never got to be on the same teams, however, for any class competitions. We were always separated to keep the teams fair.

This was the first time I had ever had a female gym teacher. All through elementary school my gym teachers had been men. Mrs. Falls was in her forties, had blonde curly hair, and wore a crisp white blouse and tailored shorts. She had a swarthy complexion and always wore bright red lipstick, which I thought was odd for a gym teacher. She had a raspy voice which initially gave an impression of gruffness, but she was far from that. She was kind and encouraging, even to the girls who hated gym class. She enjoyed teaching different sports. I loved everything about her, and after one month at Conroy Junior High School I knew that I wanted to grow up and be a gym teacher like Mrs. Falls. That would be *after* my professional basketball career was finished, of course. At least I now recognized I had an option if professional basketball didn't work out. Up to this point I never realized that being a gym teacher was a career option for women.

Mrs. Falls told me to continue striving to excel in sports and go to college. She said, "Debbie, you have talents and skills running out of your ears! We need good female physical educators." I was lucky to have Mrs. Falls for both seventh- and eighth-grade physical education. Her classes were the highlight of my two years at Conroy Junior High.

It was frustrating to only have gym class as a place to display my sports talents at school. Throughout my two years in junior high school, my girlfriends and I would attend many of the boys' sporting events--- football, basketball, wrestling, baseball, and track. We would sit in the bleachers and cheer for them. Many of the girls would talk about how cute certain boys were. I thought they were cute, too, but I wanted desperately to be on the fields and courts competing. I felt unfulfilled.

One day in the school library I found a book titled *"I Always Wanted to Be Somebody."* It was the autobiography of Althea Gibson, a black woman who had won many national and international tennis tournaments, including Wimbledon. I was fascinated by her story of success as a black female in a predominantly "white" sport. Even more impressive was that she earned money for playing tennis. I knew nothing about tennis and didn't own a tennis racket, but I thought that it might be a sport in which I could excel since I was good at every sport I tried. The only tennis courts I had seen in our town were at the high school, too far away for me to ride my bike, and at a country club on the edge of town. I asked my mom about the possibly of taking tennis lessons. She told me that the only tennis lessons she was aware of were offered at the country club, which we could not afford. I had read in her autobiography that Althea Gibson had not paid for tennis lessons as a young girl. She had an interested mentor who took Althea under his wing and taught her tennis at her local playground in Harlem. Unfortunately, a majority of the playgrounds in Indiana had basketball courts rather than tennis courts. It was disappointing because I would have liked to learn to play tennis.

*****

A carnival came to town one week in the late spring of eighth grade and I got permission from my parents to go with my best girlfriend, Margie Speck. It was Friday night and Margie had permission to spend the night at my house after the carnival. Sleepovers with special friends were a big part of socialization during junior high school. Most of my girlfriends didn't play sports, but we'd watch television, listen to records, and talk about the boys at our school.

Mom drove us to the carnival and handed me $5 to spend on rides and games. It was fun to feel grown-up enough to be unchaperoned for the evening. The carnival midway was a blaze of bright lights and colors. The aroma of caramel corn, hot dogs, and barbeque filled the air. Children carried huge tufts of pink and blue cotton candy attached to narrow paper funnels. The grinding sounds of generators powering the rides, and the squeals from riders turning upside down and sideways caused my heart to race with excitement. Hawkers yelled from their booths beckoning us to throw rings and balls at moving targets. Popping sounds could be heard from the shooting galleries. Stuffed animals, dolls, and various prizes hung from the booths as an enticement to play. Margie and I saw a group of boys from our school. They were trying to toss nickels into glass jars for prizes. We stood and watched them for awhile, but when it appeared that they were embarrassed since none of them were winning, we continued to walk down the midway.

We stopped in front of a basketball-shooting booth and watched some high school boys trying to make baskets. Their shots were hitting the rim and bouncing off with loud clanks. The sign read: **3 SHOTS FOR 25¢. MAKE ALL 3 AND WIN A BEAR.** Margie looked at me and opened her eyes wide with excitement. "Debbie, why don't you try to win a bear?" she asked.

A man wearing a green baseball cap with "John Deere" embroidered on the front overheard her and leaned toward us. "You know those rims are smaller than normal and they make the rims tighter than a tick.

It's really hard to make a basket. You have to be dead on."

His words fueled my competitive fire. I pulled my ponytail a little tighter and unbuttoned my jacket to allow my arms to move freely. I moved to the counter and slapped down a quarter.

"I wanna try," I said to the hawker.

The hawker was old, with rough, wrinkled skin. His nose was pointed like a rat's and he squinted at me while he ran his fingers through his greasy gray hair. He was holding a small megaphone that he twirled with one finger when he wasn't shouting into it.

"Well, well! Let's see what the little lady can do!" he shouted through his megaphone as he pocketed my quarter.

He handed me a ball. It was rubbery, unlike the leather balls that I usually used. It reminded me of a bouncy playground ball. I positioned my hands carefully on the ball, gripping the seams with my fingertips. I eyed the basket, calculating the height and distance in my head. The distance seemed a little farther than a free throw, so I jumped a little as I launched my shot. It passed cleanly through the net.

"Wow, we've got a player here," the hawker shouted toward the midway.

He handed me another ball. I took aim and sank the next shot. Margie slapped me on the back, jumping up and down with excitement.

"One more, little lady, and you've got yourself a prize," the hawker yelled.

A small crowd had gathered behind me. I took a deep breath and calmly launched the third shot. The ball slipped in over the front of the rim and dropped through the net. The crowd cheered and the hawker handed me a large black and white bear that was at least half my height. I handed the bear to Margie and dug into my pocket for another quarter.

"I wanna play again," I said to the hawker, placing the quarter on the counter.

The hawker made a wide sweeping motion to the growing crowd behind me and hollered, "See how easy this game is? Even a little girl can win! Yessiree, little lady, show everyone how easy it is."

My heart was pounding as I launched three more shots that ripped through the net, barely touching the rim. I pointed to a blue bear this time. The shock was evident on the hawker's face as he handed me the second bear. The crowd clapped and cheered. A blonde, curly-haired boy standing next to me handed me a quarter. He looked to be about seven years old.

"Will you shoot for me, miss?" he asked. His eyes were wide with anticipation. Margie was delirious with laughter by now.

"Sure," I said to the little boy.

As I handed the hawker the quarter, his demeanor changed dramatically. He was suddenly curt. "Two's the limit, lady," he growled.

Hearing his words, the crowd booed. I complained to him that it was not fair, because I saw no sign designating a limit. He turned away from me and took a quarter from another shooter. I shrugged my shoulders and handed my blue bear to the little boy.

"Here, I only need one bear. You can have this one." The little boy hugged the bear and beamed.

Margie and I pushed our way through the crowd and heard from various spectators.

"Good job!"

"You're better than most guys!"

"Congratulations!"

"You showed him!"

"You shoot like a boy!"

Hearing the last comment, Margie turned to the man and shouted back to him, "No! She shoots like a *basketball player*.....a *girl* basketball player!"

Margie and I giggled as we made our way down the midway, taking turns carrying my big black and white bear.

"That was cool," Margie exclaimed. "I can't wait to tell everyone in school on Monday."

I draped my arm around Margie's shoulder.

"That was a blast!" I said.

When Mom picked us up, I told her about the shooting booth, how much fun it had been to win the bears, and how the hawker had cut me off from winning any more prizes. She laughed and shook her head side to side.

"Only *you* could do that, Debbie."

Driving toward our house, music poured out of the car radio, and we sang along: **"She loves you, yeah, yeah, yeah. She loves you, yeah, yeah, yeah......"** After basketball, my next love was the Beatles. I knew the words to every one of their songs. Margie and I took turns dancing the bear on our laps with the beat of the music in the back seat. Mom tapped her hand on the steering wheel while she smoked her cigarette. Life was good.

Suddenly Mom reached forward and turned down the radio. "Oh, I forgot to tell you this afternoon,

Debbie. Dad's taking a new job and we'll be moving at the end of the school year."

I let the bear fall to the floor and Margie and I looked at each other.

"Noooooo!" we cried out simultaneously.

CHAPTER 5

FADING DREAMS

It was a new Indiana town, new school, and the same discomfort of trying to belong. Being a teenager was hard enough, but having to constantly go through the pain of finding and developing new friendships made it even more difficult. I often felt isolated. Growing up without close, long-term friendships was painful and lonely. And, as a girl, I didn't have any sports teams to join that would hasten the process of socialization. Cliques had already been established in the ninth grade at my new high school. Most of the students had gone through elementary and junior high school together. They were now ninth-grade comrades against the upperclassmen, whereas I was a single soldier in an unforgiving war of adolescence. Mom and Dad had delivered the same speech about how lucky I was to be able to learn how to adjust to new places and develop confidence in meeting new people. If it was so great, I wondered, why did I have a stomachache every morning before school?

I did look forward to gym class. At least in the gyms of the world I found equality. The basketball goals were always ten feet high and the free throw line was unfailingly fifteen feet from the basket. These seemed to be the only consistencies in the schools I attended. My new gym teacher was not at all like Mrs. Falls. Miss Garrett looked more like a man than a woman. She had short-cropped hair that lacked style. No lipstick or earrings adorned her face. A sleeveless T-shirt and baggy nylon shorts were her daily uniform. She had big breasts, so I at least knew she was a woman. With a whistle around her neck and a clipboard in her hand, she conducted the class like a military boot camp. She liked me because I was a good athlete, but she yelled at the other girls a lot and called them "prissy." I still liked gym class, but wondered why Miss Garrett walked and talked like a man. She slapped me on the butt a lot and told me that she appreciated seeing a good athlete for once.

One day when we were completing our basketball unit, Miss Garrett told me that some of the male teachers wanted to watch me shoot. I saw my math, science, and social studies teachers standing in the doorway of the gym while I drained ten jump shots in a row from various spots on the court. They were chatting with each other as they watched me. As I shot free throws, my math teacher, Mr. Carter, approached me from the group.

"Hey Debbie, next Friday at the freshman assembly, the men faculty are playing an exhibition game against the boys' ninth-grade basketball team. How would you like to play on our team?"

I grabbed the basketball as it dropped through the net and held it against my hip. I couldn't believe what I was hearing.

"You want me to play on *your* team? The faculty team?"

"Yeah, we think it would be fun to see you play against the boys, but on *our* team. You're as good, if not better, than most of the boys, and you'll be our surprise weapon."

"That will be cool!" I exclaimed.

He walked back toward the other men and they waved to me and smiled.

During the days leading up to the assembly I was overwhelmed with a myriad of emotions---excitement, nervousness, elation, worry. The only other people who knew about the game were my parents. They were excited for me and Mom promised to go to the assembly to watch. Dad was sorry that he wouldn't be able to get away from work to attend. I kept the secret from my classmates but I had trouble concentrating in my classes. I wondered how my classmates would react. Would the boys on the team be embarrassed, mad, or supportive? Would the girls make fun of me, be thrilled for me, or be jealous that I was rubbing elbows and butts with cute boys? I decided that I had to be true to myself and disregard what others thought, but I was haunted by the idea of walking the fine line between being laughed at or applauded by my peers. I did, however, have total confidence in my ability to play basketball with the best of them.

When Friday afternoon came, I sat on the bench in the boys' locker room with the men teachers as they discussed the game's strategy. We all wore navy blue shorts and white T-shirts. I idolized some of these teachers and was amazed that they had accepted a fourteen-year-old girl as their teammate. I nervously tightened the rubber band on my pony tail as I heard the students stomping their feet on the bleachers in the nearby gymnasium. It seemed like my heart was pounding equally as loud. I listened intently as the teachers instructed me on what my role would be.

"Debbie, stay on the exterior on offense, play defense against the boys' point guard, and shoot whenever you're open and in your range," Mr. Carter instructed.

The spectators went crazy as we jogged out of the locker room and began warming up with lay ups. Most of my classmates stood and pointed, laughed, and cheered when they saw me.

"Look, it's Debbie Millbern!" I heard them shout.

The boys' team stopped their warm-ups to stare at me. I glanced at them out of the corner of my eye as I went through the warm-up drills. I looked up at the bleachers and waved to my mom who was sitting next to the assistant principal. *This is going to be fun,* I thought.

The faculty team controlled the tip, but Greg Conner, who sat next to me in science class, stole the ball immediately from Mr. Carter. I squatted down into my defensive stance. Greg drove for the basket and put up a shot. Mr. Bowles, my social studies teacher, grabbed the rebound. I did exactly what the men had told me to do on the first defensive rebound. I sprinted down court toward our basket, caught a long pass from Mr. Bowles over my shoulder, and laid the ball up into the basket for the first points of the game. They crowd went crazy! I noticed that the female teachers who were sitting together were jumping and cheering the loudest. I had the crowd on my side.

The game was close, and our faculty team won by three points. I scored eight points---three field goals and two free throws. Greg had fouled me hard when I drove toward the basket. When I trotted to the free throw line to shoot, Greg walked by and whispered to me.

"Sorry, Debbie," he said.

I smiled at him and proceeded to sink the two free shots.

After the game I was surrounded by my girlfriends. They chattered about how I had made them proud. Greg and the other boys on the team shook my hand and told me what a good player I was.

That night I had a difficult time going to sleep. The sounds of the crowd and the feelings I had felt while competing wouldn't evaporate in my brain. I decided that if nothing else good happened this year at school, I wouldn't care. In fact, I told God at the end of my prayer that if he planned for me to die tonight, that would be okay, because today I had tasted heaven.

*****

Mrs. Middlebury announced in my ninth-grade English class that we were to write an essay entitled "What I Want to Be When I Grow Up." That would be easy for me because I knew exactly what I was going to do. As I wrote my essay that evening, I described in detail how I would use my basketball talents to become a professional player. I had already worked hard to develop my skills, so it would just be a matter of time before I'd grow taller and stronger. In the meantime, I'd keep fine-tuning my skills. I added to the essay that I would also like to play on the Women's U. S. Olympic Basketball Team and earn a gold medal for my country. I had recently read a story about Wilma Rudolph, a great female track star who had won three gold medals in the 1960 Olympics. I wasn't interested in track, but it had opened my eyes to the Olympics as a possibility for me.

Mrs. Middlebury returned our graded essays a few days later. To my delight, a huge A- was written boldly in red at the top of the paper. As I turned to the second page, however, my mood changed dramatically. I stared at the words Mrs. Middlebury had written at the bottom of the page: *Debbie, very good composition. However, you can never be a professional basketball player or be on an Olympic Basketball Team. There are no such teams for girls. With your athletic talents you might want to switch to cheerleading.*

As I reread her words, my head began to throb and my hands shook. I felt like I was going to pass out. Reality was slapping me in the face. It was becoming clear that my only passion, my life's dream, was never going to be fulfilled. My dream was a mere illusion subscribed by my naiveté. My calculated plan of being a professional athlete and Olympian, fueled by a dogged belief in possibilities, was disappearing like used bath water swirling down a drain.

The remainder of the school day I did not talk to anyone. I was grieving to the point of suffocation, and cried as I walked home alone from school. I lamented that my only remaining option was to become a gym teacher like Mrs. Falls. I was so tired of everyone telling me to try cheerleading.

*****

Our neighbor across the street often sat on his front porch and watched me shoot baskets in our driveway. Jerry was a little older than my parents and always had a beer in one hand and a cigarette in the other. He had bright red cheeks and thinning brown hair. One day he walked across the street and handed me a shiny booklet. It was a program from a basketball game. On the front of the program was a picture of ten red-headed women wearing red- and white-striped silk shorts and jerseys and white high-top sparkly basketball sneakers. Several were twirling basketballs on their fingertips. Behind them was a stretch limousine with the words "All-American Redheads" printed along the entire length of the car.

Jerry took a swig of his beer. "I thought you might like to look at this. I was on a business trip last week in Texas, and I went to see these gals play. They beat a team of men."

My eyes grew wide as I stared at the picture.

"Go ahead and keep it. I don't need it anymore," he said.

Thanking Jerry, I ran over to sit in the grass underneath a silver maple tree in our yard. A squirrel scurried up the tree above my head. The cool, soft grass felt like silk against my bare legs. I opened the program and read with fascination the profile of every player. They were in their twenties and traveled all over the country in the limousine. They played basketball against men as fundraisers for various community organizations. Most of the women were from Texas, Georgia, or Mississippi. I read every word of the program and studied every picture. There were pictures of the women signing autographs, and performing ball-handling demonstrations. There were pictures of cheering crowds. I was mesmerized. I folded the program and ran into the house. Mom was sorting laundry on the kitchen table.

"Mom, have you ever heard of the All-American Redheads?"

She glanced at the program and shook her head. "No, I don't believe so."

"I'd like to be an All-American Redhead after I graduate from high school. Do you suppose that you have to have red hair to make the team?"

Mom laughed. "Most of them probably dye their hair." Without hesitating Mom continued, "You can't be on that team though, because you'll be going to college after high school."

"I know. But I wouldn't have to go to college right away. I could play with the Redheads for a few years first." I studied her face to read her reaction.

"Don't plan on it," she said as she folded socks.

Dejected, I walked to my room and hopped onto my bed. I laid my head on the pillow and began reading through the program again. Thoughts swirled in my mind: *These are real women basketball players. They get paid. They travel. They wear fancy uniforms, and they have a real coach. They even play against men!* I couldn't believe that there was such a team and wondered why I hadn't heard of them. Before long I was asleep, dreaming about playing for the All-American Redheads.

*****

Boys had always been important in my life. Boys were my neighborhood buddies and my teammates on the playground. I played all kinds of sports with and against them and I lived in a house with three brothers. Now that I was in high school my view of boys was changing. I wanted to have a boyfriend. A girl's first boyfriend is special.

Eric was slightly taller than me, had light brown hair, and a broad smile. He had the whitest teeth that I had ever seen, and freckles across the bridge of his nose. He had asked me to the ninth-grade dance, and I was thrilled. Applying a little make up and wearing attractive clothes became a little more important than it had in the past, but it wasn't an obsession. Eric and I would go to the movies, hold hands, and talk about school. Since we were too young to drive, we would ride our bikes to a soda shop for milkshakes. I knew nothing about love, but he had told me several times how pretty I was and how much he liked me. I enjoyed being with Eric and felt socially accepted since I had a boyfriend like all of the other popular girls. Eric would carry my books for me after school, which was a sign to our classmates that we were a "couple." Eric made me feel special.

One Saturday afternoon Eric and I were watching television at my house and decided to go outside to shoot baskets in our driveway. We were casually shooting and laughing when he suggested that we play one-on-one. For the first time in my life I felt conflicted by playing against a boy. I knew that I was a better basketball player than Eric, so a whirlwind of scenarios flashed through my brain. *What if I win? Will he still like me? Will he like me for being the athlete that I am, or will he feel belittled? If I let him win, will I be mad at myself for giving in? Should I compete my hardest and take a chance of appearing unfeminine, or will he appreciate my skills? Maybe I should refuse to play him, but that would be denying my innermost competitive nature.*

I decided letting him win would be like telling a white lie. You know.....when someone calls you when you're asleep and they ask, "Did I wake you?" And you respond "No." Or when someone asks, "Does this dress make me look fat?" And you also respond with a convincing "No." We all tell white lies to protect someone's feelings. Should I try to protect Eric's feelings?

I thought back to an episode of *Father Knows Best* on television in which the youngest daughter, Kathy, had been counseled by her father on how to deliberately lose a competitive event against a boy. Her father had warned Kathy about the consequences of damaging a male ego. Male ego? I was shocked. Why should she care about that? That scene seemed silly to me at the time, but I now found myself wavering in the same social and cultural conundrum that Kathy faced. I was confused. My mom was a better bridge player than my dad. She was better at *Scrabble* and also a better cook. Women were better than men at many tasks, so why were women expected to be inferior in sports? If women happen to be superior at something, how does that shatter a male ego?

As these thoughts were swirling in my head, Mom stepped outside to tell Eric that his mother had called and wanted him to come home. Eric hopped on his bike and headed down the street, shouting back to me. "Maybe we can play on another day, Debbie."

I waved back to Eric and felt a wave of relief. I still had a boyfriend, but I wondered for how long.

I never had the opportunity to go one-on-one against Eric. Dad made yet *another* dinnertime announcement that he was taking *another* new job, so we began preparing to move in a few months. Like a shooting star, my ninth-grade year was gone in the blink of an eye. After a tearful good-bye to Eric and my other friends, we left town. Eric cried and told me that he'd love me forever. I wasn't sure what love was, but my heart ached anyway.

<u>CHAPTER 6</u>

FINALLY....ON A REAL TEAM

The literal meaning of "sophomore" is "wise fool," being interpreted as a person with some knowledge, but still immature---thus, a fool. I was attending my seventh school in ten years of formal schooling, and I felt like a fool (and not a wise one). I was numb to the excitement and anticipation that most new school years bring. I was tired of working at making new friends who already had established "best friends" from years before. I also felt a hesitancy to get emotionally close to people, fearing that I would have to leave them again as I had so many times in the past. The teachers at Nappanee High School seemed to already know a lot of the students in my classes. As my new teachers went through their class lists on the first day, they spoke of my classmates' brothers, sisters, and parents. With me, they merely called out my name and executed a quick glance my way. I missed my old friends. Many of my "best friends" of the past had vowed to stay in touch after we moved, but they didn't. Not even Eric.

The school did have an organization that excited me. It was called the Girls Athletic Association or G.A.A. It was an intramural sports program that met two times a week after school for various sports competitions. I enjoyed playing soccer, volleyball, basketball, and softball with the girls in my school and soon became recognized within the club for my athletic abilities. G.A.A. also became a primary social outlet for me to develop new friendships with girls who had a similar interest in playing sports. It was the first time in my life that I was able to develop a comradeship with other girl athletes my age.

On some Saturdays our G.A.A. would meet with other high schools' G.A.A. organizations for a "play day." All of the girls from various schools would be mixed together for a full day of competition. I thought it was odd that we didn't stick with our own schoolmates to form a team to compete against other schools. That was unlike our boys' high school sports teams that had extensive competitive schedules against nearby schools. I asked the female teacher who served as our G.A.A. sponsor why we couldn't play as a single team against other schools. She responded, "Because you girls shouldn't be too competitive. You should only play for fun."

"That's ridiculous," I replied. "Why play a sport if you don't try your hardest to win together as a team?"

She shrugged her shoulders and walked away.

Play days soon became boring to me. The girls laughed and giggled too much while playing, and the competition was weak. I scored 45 points in one basketball game. Like Moses parting the Red Sea, the girls simply got out of my way as I dribbled toward the basket. I believed in the fun of developing friendships while playing, but the real fun for me was meeting a challenge and pushing as hard as possible to compete.

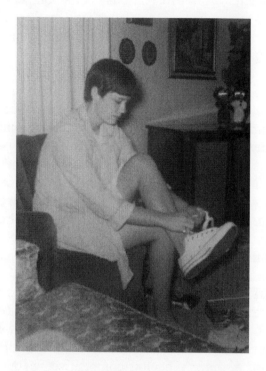

Always on my Christmas lists . . . new basketball shoes.

*****

"Just shoot me," I yelled at my parents as they announced another move. High school number three was now on my radar screen. I was getting ready to start my junior year. Prayerful words welled up inside me. *Please God, why can't I have a normal high school experience like everyone else? How will I ever survive another new school?*

Whereas all of the other Indiana towns in which we had previously lived were small or mid-sized, our new home was in a large industrial city across the Ohio River from Louisville, Kentucky. Jeffersonville High School covered an entire city block in the center of the downtown. On the first day of school, the Dean of Girls came into our English class and asked every girl to kneel on the floor so that she could measure the length of our skirts. Our hems could be no more than two inches from the ground from our kneeled position. That set the tone of hard-core rules and regulations at this school. No loitering in the halls. No trips to the bathroom during class. No excuses for tardiness. They did provide a smoking area for students outside in a courtyard. It was packed during the lunch hour.

The building was very old and dark. Every concrete step, inside and out, had a curvature to it, indicating years of wear from thousands of students scurrying up and down the stairways. Cracked, gray concrete floors in the hallways were heavily waxed, making them the only shiny feature in the building. The clouded glass windows were imbedded with wire mesh and looked like they had a hundred years of grime on them. The student population was very diverse and the noise was deafening in the hallway between classes. All I could think about was getting through each day.

I was enrolled in advanced classes, so my classmates were friendly and bright. But, of course, they had all been in school together for ten years, so I was an outsider. I worked hard in my classes and established a reputation among my classmates and teachers as a good student. I had one central goal. It was to endure the next two years of high school and get to college to study to become a gym teacher like Mrs. Falls. I realized that playing professional basketball was not going to happen, so I had resigned myself to the only career that would allow women to be involved in sports---a physical education teacher.

One day after taking a test in chemistry class, my teacher called me to his desk. Mr. McCain was a crusty old man with crooked yellow teeth. He smelled like tobacco and often wore mismatched socks. It was hard to overlook the tiny hairs growing out of his nostrils and ears. When he laughed he made a high-pitched snorting sound. Even though he was weird, I liked chemistry and had the top grades in the class. Looking up from the stack of tests that he was grading, Mr. McCain handed me my test. It had a large red A+ at the top.

"What are you going to do after graduation, Debbie?" he asked.

Without hesitation I proudly announced that I was going to become a gym teacher.

His mouth dropped open as he stared at me. He wrinkled his nose and slowly shook his head from side to side. "But you're such a good student! What a waste of your life that will be!" He stared at me a few more seconds then looked down and resumed grading, still shaking his head.

I stood motionless, feeling like I was paralyzed. I struggled to find the words to defend myself. To me, becoming a gym teacher would be a respectable career. How else could I utilize my love for sports and my athletic talent? In silence, I turned and walked back to my desk trying to think how my former beloved gym teacher, Mrs. Falls, might have responded.

*****

Because our high school was so large, the boys' sports teams were among the best in the state. Since there were no sports teams for girls, I joined the girls' cheerblock. From our huge blocked section in the bleachers, we performed synchronized arm motions and held cards to flash massive jigsaw pictures during the boys' football and basketball games. I still viewed cheerleading as a position of subservience, but being a member of the cheerblock gave me some sense of belonging in my new school. I enjoyed socializing with the girls who sat around me. However, because of some new family responsibilities, the cheerblock became my only school extracurricular activity. Dad had bought me an old Ford Falcon sedan with a manual transmission. Since I had recently gotten my driver's license, the Falcon became my transportation to and from school each day. It was exciting to have my own "wheels," but there was one hitch. Since Mike was away at college and money was tight, Mom had taken a job as a bookkeeper in a local factory. It was now my responsibility to transport my younger brothers to and from their schools every day. They attended different schools, so I had to dash out of my last class each day in order to drive to their schools. I was then expected to stay with them until Mom got home from work. I dearly loved my little brothers. They were great kids and I enjoyed being with them. However, my responsibilities to them meant that I could not participate in any clubs or events that occurred immediately after school. It was a cruel trade-off for having a driver's license and my own car, and I felt even more isolated from my classmates. College couldn't come soon enough as far as I was concerned.

*****

One of my teachers stopped me in the hallway one day and told me about a women's basketball league that was being organized across the river in Louisville. Most of the teams were made up of women from factories and various businesses. They played their games in church gymnasiums and recreation centers throughout the city on Tuesday nights. He gave me the telephone number of one of the business owners who was looking for more players for his team. That evening I pleaded with my parents to allow me to try out for the team. Because the games were at night and after my babysitting duties, Mom and Dad gave me permission to join the league. I figured they felt a little guilty that I was deprived of attending most of my school's extracurricular activities except for the Friday and Saturday night football and basketball games.

After a practice session one Saturday afternoon at the St. Nicholas Church in Louisville, I became a member of the Lucas Brothers Plumbing women's basketball team. I was seventeen, whereas most of the women on the team were in their late twenties and early thirties. They drank, swore, smoked, and played rough. Many of them looked and acted like men, arriving at the games dressed in jeans, overalls, flannel shirts, baseball caps, and heavy boots. They carried wallets in their hip pockets and keys attached to their belts. Our team uniforms were bright purple with yellow numbers. The front of the shirt had a picture of a faucet with the words *"Lucas Brothers Plumbing"* imprinted underneath it. It was exciting to have a real uniform. My teammates were Bess, Ollie, Moe, Tiny, Phyllis, Billie, and Sammie. They adopted me as if I was their daughter and I loved the intense competitions we faced together. Whereas I played with finesse and skill, they played rugged and physical. I soon became the leading scorer in the eight-team league and my teammates protected me as much as they could from the elbows, trippings, and knees from opponents. I was bruised and sore after most games but couldn't wait for the next Tuesday when I'd drive my Falcon across the Ohio River to another battle on the hardwood. After each game, the women on various teams would gather in the parking lot or a nearby bar to drink beer and smoke while I hurried home to do my homework.

My parents could tell from my enthusiasm how much fun I was having. Playing on this team filled the void of loneliness and misery I was experiencing at school. This was my first real team, and even with its craziness, it began to soothe my perpetual ache to play. I existed for Tuesday nights. During classes I often doodled basketball plays in my notebook. X's and O's were aligned beside my notes on Shakespeare and the Battle of the Bulge. I didn't tell Mom and Dad too many details about my teammates or opponents, knowing that they might not be as enthusiastic as I was about the people or the playing environment.

One Tuesday evening in January my dad had the night off from his retail job and told me that he'd like to come to my game. I was apprehensive and anxious, but also thrilled that he would finally see me play. That night we were scheduled to play at an inner-city factory whose recreation center had a basketball court painted on a slick concrete floor. It had two vertical steel beams in the middle of the playing court, located near the top of each free throw circle. There was a rickety set of bleachers along one wall, with the lowest row extending about a foot into the court.

I drove Dad to the game through the snow-covered city streets that glistened as if thousands of diamonds were imbedded in white frosting. I was excited! It was so cold inside the recreation center that Dad and the few other spectators didn't remove their coats. Dad took a seat near the end of the bleachers.

Once the game started I could hear Dad's voice. He shouted instructions to my teammates and me. His encouragements made me play harder. Soon he began standing and yelling at the referees about missed calls. He yelled at our opponents. His comments could be heard all over the gym. Whenever I got pushed hard or elbowed, he'd scream, "Foul!" I was excited that he was into the game, yet I was also somewhat embarrassed that he was so much louder than the other spectators.

Since there was no visible time clock in the gym, the time keeper pulled a large comb out of his huge Afro hairdo and threw it onto the middle of the floor to signal that it was half-time. We stopped playing and my team assembled in the hall near the restroom to talk about our second-half strategy. I flinched as I saw a cockroach scurry into an empty Coke bottle lying on the floor close to where I was sitting.

Dad continued his yelling during the second half. I was becoming oblivious to it. Once while guarding an opponent, she intentionally dribbled so close to one of the steel beams that I slammed into it and fell hard to the floor. I heard my dad scream his loudest. "That should be illegal!"

The shrill of the referee's whistle filled the air and everyone stopped playing. There was complete silence in the gym. The referee ran over to the bleachers and stood directly in front of my dad. Vigorously shaking his finger at Dad, the referee yelled, "One more word out of you, mister, and you're outta here." The referee swung his arm across his body and pointed to the side door illuminated by a large red exit sign.

I snickered while Ollie ran over and slapped me on the back.

"I love your dad!" she laughed.

"So do I!" I replied.

Dad was calm during the remainder of the game. After the game Dad came onto the court and gave me a big hug. I had scored 23 points. He was beaming.

"You are one heck of a player, Debbie! I am so proud of you!"

I grinned and wiped the perspiration from my forehead. Words could not describe the amount of happiness that oozed from every cell of my body after hearing his compliments.

Ollie approached us. Her wild Shirley Temple-like hairdo was held in place by a ragged red bandana. She pulled off her bandana and used it to twist off the bottle cap of a Pabst Blue Ribbon beer. She held the bottle out to my dad.

"Here, Mr. Millbern, have a beer on me."

I attempted to hide my expression of panic as I looked at my dad. He laughed and shook Ollie's hand, politely declining her kind offer.

Dad wrapped his arm around my shoulders as we walked outside into the wintry night. The cold air took my breath away as we hurried toward the Falcon. Dad climbed into the passenger seat and quickly slammed the door. I pushed in the clutch on the Falcon and listened to the engine grind as I turned the key in the ignition. Like an indignant child the engine moaned and finally rolled over. We sat shivering in silence while the engine warmed to a soft hum and the defroster slowly melted the ice on the windshield. Dad turned to me, the cold vinyl seat creaking under his weight.

"That was really fun!" he exclaimed. I looked at him and grinned. After a few moments of silence, he continued with a heightened tone of enthusiasm, "So....when's your next game?" His blue eyes sparkled in the moonlight and he had a huge smile on his face. I reached over and grasped his chilly hand and squeezed it three times. He responded with four squeezes.

*****

Graduation finally arrived and I spent an enjoyable summer playing on a slow-pitch softball team with some of the same women with whom I had played basketball. I would soon be leaving for Indiana University to study physical education. Whereas most students entering such a large university would be filled with trepidation, I felt none. To me it was simply another move. But this time it was exciting. I was transitioning to freedom and new opportunities. I was also moving to a place where I would stay for at least four years, longer than any other place in which I had lived. That was exciting in itself!

The 1960s were coming to a close, and I had come of age in one of the most historically and culturally complex decades of all time. The Civil Rights Movement had created enormous tension in our country. The passage of the Civil Rights Act in 1964 had changed the future for African-Americans. The Cuban Missile Crisis and Cold War had resulted in fear and the mass construction of home bomb shelters. In every school I attended we practiced bomb drills by crouching under our desks and covering our heads at the sound of a loud siren blasting through the hallways. In fact, Mom and Dad had drilled into our heads a location where our family was to meet if our country was attacked and we happened to be separated.

We experienced the shocking assassinations of President John F. Kennedy, his brother Robert, and Martin Luther King, Jr. On live television we watched Lee Harvey Oswald, the accused assassin of President Kennedy, shot and killed by Jack Ruby as he was being transferred to jail. While watching JFK's funeral on television, I saw my parents cry for the very first time. And now the Vietnam War was escalating by the day. Just weeks after my high school graduation ceremony, we gathered around our television and watched a man land on the moon. Because of television, the events of the world were brought into the living rooms in our small, idyllic Midwest towns. Walter Cronkite told us "the way it was" and *I Love Lucy* kept us laughing.

Despite the violence and fear of the '60s, I had been inspired by John F. Kennedy's inauguration speech.

"Let the word go forth . . . that the torch has been passed to a new generation."

"Ask not what your country can do for you; ask what you can do for your country."

I was equally inspired by Martin Luther King, Jr.'s *"I Have a Dream"* speech.

The events we experience and witness during our youth help mold us for the rest of our lives. These events define us. I was emerging from my mold as a self-assured, confident young woman with a major streak of independence and competitiveness. My mother had been correct that my transient childhood would make me strong. The lessons I learned and the struggles I endured while trying to be accepted as a female athlete were now part of my DNA.

Paralleling the societal changes for equal rights for African-Americans were expanded opportunities for women in general. The roles of women in the workplace, academic world, and political arena were changing. Consequently, I was beginning to read in the newspapers about more women athletes. Billie Jean King was a successful professional tennis player. There were professional women golfers. The Olympic Games were expanding to offer more women's competitions (still no basketball, however). Yet there were also some discrepancies that confused me. For example, whereas Billie Jean King had won three Wimbledon singles titles and was financially supporting her law student husband, she could not get a credit card unless it was in her husband's name. She was both a heroine and a prisoner of the times!

In 1967, Kathrine Switzer registered as "K. V. Switzer" to run the Boston Marathon. Almost three miles into the race, an angry race official jumped off the media truck and tried to forcibly remove Kathrine from the race after realizing that she was a woman. Marathon races were regarded as "men-only" competitions.

"Get the hell out of my race!" the official screamed at her. With the help of her boyfriend, Kathrine pulled away from the official and finished the race.

Another restriction that confused me was the fact that women track athletes were not allowed to compete in distances over 800 meters in the Olympic Games. The thought was that long distance running could harm a woman's reproductive organs and make her infertile. And, outside of these limited competitive arenas there were still no female sports journalists or television reporters. Despite these confusing inconsistencies and inequalities, I had hope for the future.

*****

At dinner just weeks before I was to leave for college, Dad announced that he, my mom, and my two younger brothers would be moving to Columbus, Ohio. For once, I didn't care. I felt bad for my brothers who were entering middle and high school, but this time it wouldn't affect me. I was entering college where there would be thousands of "new kids"---all freshmen. I was confident and ready to make my mark this time as the *new kid* among many. Although my dream of becoming a professional basketball player had withered, I still loved sports and was determined to become the best gym teacher in the world to thousands of young girls. Hopefully I would be as inspirational as Mrs. Falls had been to me.

CHAPTER 7

COLLEGE: A FRESH START

I estimated her to be anywhere between 60 and 100 years old. Her short gray hair looked like it hadn't been combed in days. *This woman doesn't own a mirror,* I thought to myself. She wore a white cotton blouse and a plain navy skirt that ended mid-calf. Spotless white Keds tennis shoes and thin anklet socks with scalloped trim completed her attire. She had wide hips and an ample chest. The flab on the back of her arms jiggled like Jell-O as she wrote her name on the black chalkboard. Looking over her bifocals, she slowly surveyed the classroom giving the impression that she wouldn't tolerate foolishness. Leaning against the wooden desk, she cleared her throat.

"My name is Dr. Naomi Smith, and I am the advisor for freshman physical education majors. Welcome to the Women's Physical Education Department."

I glanced around the room. Thirty pairs of eager eyes were glued to Dr. Smith.

"I have been a faculty member here for thirty-five years, and have taught every sport that you can think of."

I tried to visualize Dr. Smith doing an arabesque on a balance beam, running over a hurdle on the track, spiking a volleyball, or shooting a jump shot.

"You've got to be kidding me," I murmured under my breath. The pale, anorexic-looking girl sitting next to me giggled. She looked like a ballerina. *Must be a dance major*, I thought.

Dr. Smith continued, "I am handing out a paper with all of the particulars you need to know about securing a personal locker in the locker room, how to check out sports equipment, and where the various classrooms, gymnasiums and dance studios are located in this building. There are two important points I want you to know right now. One....you must always wear a skirt or dress in this building. If you have a sports class, you change into your athletic clothes in the locker room, and after class, change back into your dress or skirt. Two....you are training to become a physical education teacher, NOT a gym teacher or a PE teacher. You are a physical education major, NOT a phys ed major or phy ed major. Use the entire two words – *physical education* – in all of your conversations and when you write your papers for classes."

My mouth dropped open when I heard the word "skirt." My vision of living in jeans, shorts, and sweat pants over the next four years vanished.

"We have a dress code?" the girl next to me whispered, equally astounded. "This is 1969, not 1939!" she exclaimed.

I raised my hand and Dr. Smith nodded to acknowledge me.

"Dr. Smith," I politely asked. "Are we required to wear a skirt all over campus and during non-PE.....whoops....I mean non-physical education classes?"

"No. Skirts or dresses are only required in the physical education building. We want our physical education majors to look like ladies while in this building."

Once we were dismissed from the orientation session, I walked back to the dormitory with two of my new classmates. Pam was tall and pretty with a long blonde pony tail. Sandy was a short, plump brunette with tight curly hair.

"I guess they don't want us to look like a bunch of dykes," Pam said.

Sandy and I stopped and stared at Pam.

"What do you mean?" I asked.

"You know... dykes ... lesbians ... homosexuals," Pam responded.

"Lesbians? I'm not a lesbian!" Sandy exclaimed.

"Neither am I," I replied.

"Yeah, well, look around. They're thick in PE," Pam said.

"You mean in 'physical education'," I snickered as I corrected her.

We all laughed, even though it wasn't really that funny. It was more of an uneasy laugh.

"Girls, welcome to the world of physical education," Pam said. "In fact, I read a statement in one of my great-grandma's health books proclaiming that the enjoyment of physical activity was not only unfeminine, but proof of lesbianism." Sandy and I laughed nervously as we watched Pam pull open the heavy door to the dormitory lobby and disappear inside.

In reality, I was naïve. Homosexuality was a vague concept in my mind. My innocence was solidified by the times. Homosexuality was never written about in newspapers, nor discussed on television programs. I had overheard classmates in high school calling some guys "queers," but I wasn't exactly sure what they meant by it. The guys they called "queers" dressed differently and had feminine mannerisms. Many were in art or drama. Someone told me that the queers preferred to date other guys rather than girls. That confused me, and Pam's comments were equally confusing. I had never thought about *girls* wanting to date other *girls*. It was my perception that boys seemed to have other boys as "buddies," and girls had "girlfriends." I never considered those relationships to be romantic. However, I reflected back to my teammates on the Lucas Brothers Plumbing basketball team. Several of them displayed masculine characteristics, and some lived together. Were they lesbians? Or were they simply girlfriends? I had been so caught up in playing the sport that I glossed over everything else. I didn't care about their sexuality. To me they were my devoted teammates, and, besides, none of them had ever asked me on a date.

*****

Even though I suffered through wearing a skirt to the physical education building, I was in my glory. I had classes in badminton, bowling, field hockey, soccer, tennis, golf, volleyball, and folk dance. We were taught the techniques, rules, history, and strategies of each activity. And I was free to wear jeans to my calculus, English, and anatomy classes. The campus was alive with activities, dances, clubs, lectures, musical performances, sporting events, and plays. I could eat, sleep, and go out when I wanted. I enjoyed socializing with the girls in my dormitory and going to parties with them, even though we lamented about our 11:00 p.m. curfew on weeknights. On weekends we were allowed to stay out until 1:00 a.m., and guys were allowed in our dormitory lounges until 1:00 a.m. as well. I soon became friends with many of the other physical education majors, as we pursued our shared passion for sports.

One day a sign caught my eye in the physical education building. It read: **All women are invited to try out for the women's basketball team on Monday, October 15 at 4:00 p.m**. My heart skipped a beat. The university had a women's basketball team! After dinner that evening I checked out a basketball from the physical education equipment room and found an empty gym where I could practice. I dribbled up and down the court and practiced my shots from various spots. It felt good as I maneuvered around the court dodging imaginary opponents.

After a couple of hours I noticed an older, gray-haired man standing in the doorway watching me. He was tall and wore a brown suit, white shirt, and a red bow tie. He had dark-rimmed glasses and bushy gray eyebrows. He leaned casually against the door jam and watched for awhile, then disappeared. The next evening I repeated my routine of private practice, and again saw the older gentleman pause and watch me for awhile. He looked like someone's gentle grandfather, so I didn't feel afraid being alone in the gym. On the third night, the man appeared again and this time began slowly walking toward me. I stopped shooting as he approached and I glanced toward the side exit doors in case I needed to escape.

"Hello," he said, stopping about fifteen feet from me.

"Hi," I replied with a degree of hesitation.

He smiled and blinked his soft brown eyes. "I've been watching you shoot during the past week and must say that I've never seen a girl shoot a basketball as well as you do. Your form is perfect."

"Thank you," I replied. "I'm going to try out for the women's basketball team."

"Well I can say that you will most likely not only make the team, but will become a star, especially with your obvious work ethic and talent."

"That would be nice," I answered. "But I just want to play on a real team."

"What is your name?" he asked.

"Debbie Millbern," I replied.

"Well, Debbie, you keep up the good work. It's a real pleasure to watch you practice." He turned and started walking toward the exit. His brown loafers made a squeaking sound with each step on the shiny wooden floor.

"Hey," I yelled back to him. "I didn't get your name, sir."

He stopped and turned toward me. "Branch McCracken," he said as he waved good-bye.

"Nice to meet you, Mr. McCracken," I shouted to him just before he disappeared through the doorway. I thought his name sounded familiar, but couldn't place where I had heard it before. I felt pleased with his comments, however, and deemed myself ready for the tryouts.

*****

I made the basketball team and it became the most exciting experience of my life. My teammates became my second family. We had uniforms…kind of. They were actually our own red shorts that were required for all physical education majors. Then we purchased white, sleeveless tops with numbers pressed onto the fronts and backs. We had daily practices and a dedicated coach. Dr. Irene Mehnert was a tall, married woman in her mid-thirties. As a post-doctoral student at IU, she volunteered to coach us for a small stipend. Whereas Coach Mehnert had not been a basketball player, she was a strong proponent for sports for women. She was willing to learn, and we were excited to have a committed coach.

Our winter schedule consisted of twelve games against teams like Purdue, Notre Dame, Butler, and Ball State. Even though our home games were played in a small gymnasium in the physical education building, we developed a small, loyal group of fans and even got a few write-ups in the university newspaper. The gymnasium where we played did not have bleachers, so the spectators stood along the sidelines, leaning against the wall. We were responsible for washing our own uniforms and purchasing our own basketball shoes. We would pile into a van, driven by Coach Mehnert, for road trips. Most of the games were within a six-hour radius, so we would leave early in the morning, drive to the other college, play the game, and then ride back home after a quick stop at a fast-food restaurant for a post-game meal. We packed our own sandwiches or snacks for the pre-game meal. The gymnasiums where we played were not the huge arenas where the men played their games. They were often auxiliary gyms in the physical education building or recreation center. We often changed into our uniforms in a restroom. Since there was no advanced scouting of opponents, every opposing player was faceless. We knew nothing about our opposing team's offensive or defensive strategies, tendencies, or best players. Coach Mehnert would watch our opponents during their warm ups, then give instructions in our huddle before the game. "Number 40 is left-handed; number 32 is tall, so she must play in the center; number 11 rarely missed a shot during her warm up, so play her tight," she'd instruct.

What followed was the purest form of coaching, making adjustments throughout the game, during time-outs, and at half-time. We had to be prepared for anything thrown at us. Not only were we talented players, but we were like five on-the-court coaches as we communicated with each other. We played hard, and beat most teams by wide margins. I was the leading scorer.

My teammates became the sisters I never had. Like me, they were girls who grew up in towns all over Indiana desperately wanting to play basketball. None had played high school basketball. Everyone had developed their skills on playground and driveway courts against boys. Our bond was the love of playing basketball. On road trips we would laugh, and sing along with the radio. We talked about classes, our professors, and our hopes and dreams. After each game I would call my parents and give them play-by-play details. If there was a write-up in the paper, I cut it out and sent it to them. I saw Mr. McCracken at a few of our games and he often would smile and give me a "thumbs up" after I scored. I loved my physical education classes, playing basketball, and the social life on campus. It was a grand time.

There was only one aspect of our competitions that confused me. After tough, hard-fought games, we were required to assemble in a classroom or lounge to socialize with our opponents. This occurred at both "home" and "away" games. We would quickly change after the game and then meet the other players and coaches for cookies and punch. I found it awkward after battling against the "enemy" to smile and make small talk with them. It was difficult to converse with a player who twenty minutes ago was elbowing me in the ribs to get around me. No doubt our opponents felt the same way. Shaking hands after a game was one thing, but it seemed incongruous to smile and share a bowl of punch as if we were all now best friends. I felt a disconnect at these gatherings as if the outcome of the game hadn't mattered or bothered us.

Except for perhaps tennis, golf, and gymnastics, most athletic competitions for women were still viewed as abnormal and unladylike. This seemed to be especially true in team sports like basketball and softball. It was as if society could not imagine that a female athlete could be multidimensional---a tough, hard-driving player on the court or field, and yet a normal, feminine woman off the court. There seemed to be a stigma attached to women who enjoyed racing down a basketball court, crashing the boards for a rebound, or slamming a home run. Bending over and hanging on one's knees, being out of breath, and donning sweat-soaked clothes were not considered normal behaviors for a female. My guess was that the cookies-and-punch social hour was designed to keep us civilized in the eyes of society.

Regardless of the attempts to feminize athletes with social hours and skirts, I witnessed many female athletes who exhibited masculine behaviors in the way they walked, talked, dressed, and wore their hair. Since I spent a lot of time on campus eating, socializing, and studying with other female athletes and physical education majors, I often overheard groups of guys walk by us snickering and whispering the words "dykes," "lesbians," or "butches." It hurt me to be labeled and misjudged by an assumption. I wasn't about to curb my competitive instincts and physical prowess by fearing these labels, but they did bother me. It also troubled me that so many of the women athletes felt a need to act like men. My guess was that the root of these behaviors and reactions was imbedded in the cultural assumption that team sports were for men only. Women who stepped into this arena were perceived as moving outside their acceptable sphere of socialization. Therefore, looking and acting like men made these women feel more comfortable.

Even though I felt conflicted at times trying to balance competitiveness and aggressiveness with femininity, I was overall satisfied being an athlete and a woman. Even so, oftentimes on a first date, after the guy had discovered that I was on the basketball team, he would make a comment like, "Wow, you sure don't *look* like a basketball player!" My response was invariably, "Oh really? Please tell me what a basketball player is supposed to look like." And, of course, there was always a tendency for people to speculate about the sexual orientation of us "abnormal jocks." I would become especially irritated when my dates jokingly inquired about all of my "dyke" teammates. My teammates were great people and loyal friends, and I resented any disparaging comments directed toward them.

Shooting a jump shot at Indiana University

Taking it in for two more points

*****

After basketball practice one day I stayed in the gymnasium alone to shoot free throws. I loved the solitude broken only by the echo of the ball hitting the shiny wood floor and the swishing sound of the net. In a gymnasium I was alone, but not lonely. The perspiration dripping from my forehead and rolling down my back provided an uncanny sense of pleasure. I was proud of my muscles, strength, and power. Being part of a team filled me with great joy and a sense of purpose to work at being the best player that I could be.

Entering the locker room after practice, the only sound I heard was the consistent drip of water from a leaky showerhead. All of my teammates had left, so I thought. I turned the corner near my locker and was surprised to see one of my teammates, Alice Barnes, sitting on the bench in front of my locker. She had changed from her practice clothes and was wearing a green corduroy jumper and black knee socks. Her overstuffed gym bag was sitting on the floor. Alice was a junior, but rarely played in any of the games. She was tall, big-boned, and clumsy. She also suffered from a bad case of acne. She was a nice girl, but very quiet. I was in two classes with Alice---anatomy and calculus.

"Hey Alice," I said as I stepped over her bag and began turning the dial on the combination lock dangling from my locker. "What's going on?" I asked cheerfully without giving her a glance.

"Nothing," she responded in a softer than normal tone.

I sat down next to her and began unlacing my shoes. I began chatting about our anatomy class and asked her if she had finished the lab that was due the next day. She replied with a simple "yes." Trying to keep the conversation going while I kicked off my shoes and peeled off my sweaty socks, I commented about our anatomy professor and his quirky sense of humor. "Do you suppose he realizes that he has repeated the same joke about the tibia and the fibula at least three…………" I stopped abruptly as I felt Alice's hand on my thigh. She began caressing it.

"I really like you, Debbie," Alice said softly as she looked directly into my eyes.

I felt a bolt of electric energy throughout my body, as if the nerves were all charging at once. It was accompanied by a combined feeling of dread, anger, and empathy. I didn't want to overreact, but I was disturbed. I gently placed my hand on top of Alice's and carefully removed it from my leg.

"Alice, I like you too.....but not in the way that you must be hoping."

Alice sighed and dropped her head, slowly picked up her bag. She stood and I could see her cheeks blushing and tears welling in her eyes.

"I'm sorry," she whispered as she shuffled toward the door.

"So am I," I responded.

After Alice left the locker room I sat in a stupor. A cocktail of emotions was mixing in my brain. My head began to throb and my heart raced. Had I done something to lead Alice on? I tried to recall our past conversations, most of which revolved around basketball patterns or calculus formulas. The attraction of female to female beyond the point of mere friendship was still confusing to me. I had spent my entire life making friends with girls in a variety of new environments. Girls traditionally express friendship for one another in intense means that often involves hugging or holding hands or linking arms when walking. We snuggle together at slumber parties to watch movies or read books. We form an emotional intimacy as we freely share our feelings, hopes, and dreams. What had I done differently when interacting with Alice? I wondered....was this new world of athletics a unique environment that evokes intimacy in women, or could this have happened anywhere? Not only do athletes share a close emotional bond cemented by triumphs, disappointments and struggles, but our bodies are a vehicle of expression. During games we get physical by embracing each other and slapping each others' butts. We shower together. Does this closeness in mind and body elicit romantic feelings? Does this happen with men athletes?

I quickly showered and dressed, pulling the hood of my coat over my damp hair as the brisk January air met me at the exit. My head was filled with more questions than answers as I walked quickly toward my dormitory.

Alice quit the team soon after our encounter in the locker room. I never told anyone about our conversation, and I never heard the reason she gave the coach for quitting. Even though Alice and I had a few classes together, we never spoke again. I did not consciously avoid her, but whenever our eyes met, she quickly glanced away.

CHAPTER 8

SORORITY GIRL

The stately mansions that lined Third Street housed the fraternities and sororities. Their huge pillars and winding brick driveways reminded me of estates from the pages of architecture magazines. There was an aura of mystery surrounding these houses with their illuminated Greek letters prominently displayed above their giant front doors. The Greek system was relatively foreign to me. As a high school student I had visited my brother's fraternity for a weekend and remembered the house looking like a tornado had passed through leaving a residue of beer, fast food wrappers, and plastic cups. Surely the sororities would be different inside. I looked at the sorority recruitment experience as an opportunity to tour each of these beautiful mansions, and see what "sorority girls" were like.

After attending preliminary information sessions in my dormitory about the recruitment process, commonly called "rush," I discovered what a stressful event it was for many freshmen girls. Unlike me, many girls felt pressure from their families to join a certain sorority. Social standing and prestige were attached to select sororities. I listened to the girls talk about what they would wear during rush, and brag about what girls they already knew in various sororities from their high schools. Unlike most of them, I knew no one in a sorority. They chatted about Alpha Chis, Chi-Os, Thetas, and Tri-Delts. Pardon the pun, but it was all Greek to me, and I began feeling a little anxious about it, especially after my roommate announced to me that she was not going through it. "Too much pressure," she said. "And besides, I'm not pretty enough."

I'm certainly no beauty queen, I thought. Still, I decided to give it a try and stay as relaxed as possible, void of pretenses. I tricked myself into looking at sorority rush as a mere "house and garden tour." After all, I had spent my entire childhood being immersed into a similar kind of "rush" each time I entered a new school. This would be no different as I tried to determine where I fit in. I didn't have fancy clothes or long gorgeous hair like many of the girls. My short pixie cut would have to do. I was *me*, and if they didn't like *me*, so be it.

When I began attending the sorority parties and meeting the girls, I discovered that the self-assurance I had developed from my transient childhood helped. I found it easy to talk to the girls about a variety of topics. Everyone was very friendly and I loved touring the beautiful houses. As I expected, the insides of the houses were as spectacular as the outsides. The entire rush process took a week, with lists being posted nightly in the dormitory as to which girls were invited back to a house the next day for another "look." I would hear alternating screams of disappointment and excitement as girls read through the lists searching for their names. Tears flowed freely all week. The sorority girls whom I met were intelligent, interesting, and genuine. No one was an athlete, but they seemed interested in my sports background. I have to admit that as the final rush parties approached, I felt some anxiety as I was now longing to be selected. To be able to live in one of those beautiful mansions with a large group of "sisters" would be a dream. I lacked the sorority pedigree or sophistication that seemed to permeate this unique social fragment, but I felt the same yearnings for acceptance as I felt as a twelve-year-old walking into a new school.

To my surprise and delight I was invited to join one of the most prestigious and popular sororities on campus---Kappa Kappa Gamma. I was excited at the opportunity to live in a magnificent house among bright, independent, and charming young women. I had a new label - *sorority girl* - and I enjoyed getting to know seventy new "sisters." None of them were athletes, but they welcomed me as a valued member of their sorority. I felt normal and accepted.

It is interesting how our lives are like a chest of drawers, with each drawer being a particular segment of our life. I had a drawer for my family, basketball teammates, sorority sisters, classmates, and professors. I loved and appreciated each drawer as I opened them everyday.

*****

My first year in college was nearly over and I enjoyed everything about my life. I was happy with my career choice, playing on the basketball team, and joining a sorority. It had been a great year, and I looked forward to returning next fall.

Just days before I left campus for summer vacation I picked up the school newspaper and stared at the headline: *"Hall of Fame Coach Branch McCracken Dies."* On the front page was a picture of the kindly gentleman who had watched me practice in the gym at night during those first few weeks of school. I had never investigated who he was, but now the article in the paper revealed him as the retired head coach of the Indiana University men's basketball team, having coached in the '40s, '50s, and early '60s. He coached two NCAA championship teams, and had been an exceptional player before becoming a coach. He was revered by the national basketball coaching community and had been inducted into the Naismith Basketball Hall of Fame.

I felt a huge wave of regret that I had not interacted more with Coach McCracken. His complimentary and encouraging words to me now meant more than ever. I could still visualize his kind smile, deep brown eyes, and "thumbs up" signals to me. It was amazing how a brief encounter with a strange man had bolstered an unsure, yet motivated female athlete. I was sad that I never thanked him or acknowledged his own amazing accomplishments.

*****

When I returned to campus in the fall, the university felt like a comfortable shoe as I reunited with my classmates, teammates, and sorority sisters. In anticipation of the upcoming basketball season I began going to one of the gymnasiums several nights a week and playing basketball in pick-up games with college guys. They were hesitant at first to let me play, but I soon earned my place. The guys were quick and strong which helped me improve my skills.

Two weeks after returning to campus, Coach Mehnert called me. "You've been invited to try out for the Pan Am games!" she shouted into the phone.

"The *what* games?" I asked.

"There is to be a women's basketball team from the United States going to compete in the Pan American Games in Cali, Colombia, this summer, and I've talked to some people to get you a tryout for the team."

I couldn't believe what I was hearing. I couldn't speak. My voice box felt paralyzed.

"Are you still there, Debbie?" Coach Mehnert asked.

"Oh my gosh!" I shouted. "Yes! When? Where? What do I do?"

I learned that I would have to fly to Plainview, Texas, for a weekend where the coach of the team, Harley Redin, would be conducting the tryouts. I was on my own to cover the travel expenses, but Wayland Baptist College in Plainview would provide dormitory rooms in which tryout participants could stay. I was excited but also nervous about asking my parents for permission to go, *and* for money for the airplane ticket. I knew money was extremely tight for our family with me in college, my brother Mike in medical school, and my two younger brothers still living at home. Calling

Mom and Dad that evening on the phone, I explained the opportunity and how much it meant to me. They agreed to pay for a plane ticket, adding that this would be my Christmas and birthday presents this year. I thanked them at least ten times during the next five minutes and told them that they wouldn't regret it because I was confident that I could make the team. I would be playing for the great USA!

Both the campus and local newspapers wrote special articles about my upcoming tryout. I learned that the Pan American Games are held every four years, the year before each summer Olympic Games. Athletes are only from the Americas, with competitions in a wide variety of sports. Women's basketball was one of the sports included. I continued to practice vigorously on my own and against the guys at the gym since the tryout was only a few weeks away.

It was difficult to contain my excitement as I boarded the plane in Indianapolis. Oblivious to the passengers around me, I closed my eyes and visualized myself wearing a shiny red, white, and blue uniform with the letters "USA" embroidered on the front.

Plainview, Texas, was the dirtiest, dustiest place I had ever seen. Everything was sandy brown, compared to the beautiful October colors back in Indiana. Coach Redin was kind enough to pick me and another player up at the airport in his personal car. The other girl, Sue, was a player from Northern Illinois University. She and I remembered playing against each other during last year's season. I recalled her to be a very good player.

Harley Redin was a handsome man with tanned skin, thick black hair, and long sideburns. He wore a cowboy hat and snakeskin boots. He talked incessantly about the Wayland Hutcherson Flying Queens, a women's AAU basketball team that he coached. "We've won six national championships," he bragged with a Texas-like drawl.

"I didn't even know there were women's AAU basketball teams and championships," I responded.

"Of course, darlin'. We've been playing basketball in the South for years," he replied. "We travel to play teams like Nashville Business College, Hanes Hosiery, and the Raytown Piperettes. You college kids are way behind."

The other girl and I looked at each other and shrugged our shoulders, embarrassed by our ignorance. I had never heard of those teams, but now secretly wished that I had grown up in Texas. But I didn't like being called "darlin'."

The Wayland Baptist gymnasium was small, more like an ordinary high school gym in Indiana. Like everyplace in Plainview, there was a film of dust on the floor. Several huge blue and gold banners hung from the rafters declaring years of national championship glory. The banners swayed gently, a testament to the slight breeze in the otherwise stuffy gym.

"Why is your team called the Wayland Hutcherson Flying Queens?" I asked Coach Redin while sitting on the bleachers lacing up my basketball sneakers.

"Because Mr. Hutcherson owns a fleet of Beechcraft Bonanzas and he flies me and the gals to our games. He's our sponsor and number one supporter."

"Wow," I thought. "Your team is really lucky!"

As Sue and I proceeded to stretch and warm up, I wondered where the other players were. No one else had shown up. Coach Hardin blew his whistle and declared that it was time to start. For almost three hours Sue and I went through a variety of drills. We shot, jumped, dribbled, passed, ran, and played each other one-on-one. I was feeling great about my performance. I was shooting the ball well and was perfect from the free throw line. Coach Hardin sat in the bleachers shouting out instructions and keeping notes on a clipboard. Finally he stood up and said, "Okay, that's all."

Sue and I walked over to him. Sweat was dripping onto the floor from our chins and foreheads as we bent over to rest with our hands on our knees. Our shirts were so wet that they stuck to our skin.

"What about the other players? Why aren't they here at the tryout?" I asked.

"Oh, I've already seen them," he replied.

"But don't you want to see us all play with a full team, 5-on-5 full court?" I asked.

"Nope. No need for that," he replied. "You gals can catch some dinner tonight at Clara's Diner down the road. I'll be here tomorrow morning at eleven to take you back to the airport. Thanks for comin'." He made no comment about our performances.

Over dinner Sue told me that she thought we'd both had a great tryout, and had good chances of making the team. Even though I was ravenously hungry, I had a hard time swallowing my food. I told Sue that I had a feeling that this whole tryout was an illusion and that Redin probably already had his team selected. My intuition told me that *his* Wayland Hutcherson Flying Queens would make up the USA Pan American team. Even though I was exhausted, I tossed and turned in bed all night worrying about the money my parents had

spent for me to fly to this mockery of a tryout. I was
mad and hurt that my hopes for making the team were
vanishing. I felt embarrassed thinking about all the
publicity I had received back home. Everyone would
wonder why I hadn't made the team.

On the ride to the airport the next morning Coach
Redin played country music on the radio. The dust
flew around us as we sped down the road. We all spoke
very little. As he unloaded our bags at the airport
Coach Redin said, "We'll be in touch, darlin's."

Sure, I thought to myself, *don't call us. We'll call
you.*

The pain penetrated even deeper when I returned to
campus and learned the truth from Coach Mehnert. She
apologized to me for being duped, as well. My
intuition had been correct. Coach Redin selected
players from his Wayland team plus a few others from
the AAU teams with which he was familiar to make up
the USA team. Sue and I never had a chance. He only
conducted a tryout to appease a few college-level
coaches who spoke up for their players. I was
disappointed and amazed that politics had clouded the
selection of the women's national basketball team.

Mom and Dad were disappointed for me and
consoled me the best they could. They didn't seem to
be too upset, because they had been nervous about me
traveling to Colombia. Mom, however, got in one
hurtful comment that re-ignited my pain. "Traveling
that far, you *did* try your hardest, didn't you?" she
asked with a hint of sarcasm.

It felt like she had picked a scab from a healing
wound. I squeezed out a response past a lump forming

in my throat. "I gave it my all, Mom, just like I do everything," I replied as I abruptly hung up the phone.

*****

The anguish from my experience subsided as the winter came and our basketball season began. Being around my sorority sisters, practicing with my teammates, and competing in games brought me a tremendous amount of pleasure. I enjoyed my classes and professors. We had a terrific basketball season, playing against the best teams in the Midwest. My 26-points-per-game scoring average had earned me the nickname "Dead-Eye Debbie" from opponents.

At one of our games my sportsmanship and character were tested. It was a very close game with the score going back and forth during the final minutes. With the score tied and only seven seconds left in the game, there was a mad scramble of bodies for the ball on our defensive end. My teammate, Kathy, and I, along with an opposing player dove for the ball. The referee blew the whistle. The opposing player was called for a foul because she had landed on top of Kathy. The referee jogged to the scorer's bench to indicate which player had been charged with a foul. Kathy's free throws could win the game for us! As we walked down the court toward our basket, Kathy brushed up to me and nervously whispered, "I don't think I can make 'em. Shoot for me." Realizing that neither official acknowledged who had been fouled, I marched directly to the free throw line to shoot. Like most everything associated with women's collegiate sports, officiating was very rudimentary and lacked regulation. In fact, some referees were untrained volunteers. As a result, a lot of calls were missed. We players took it in stride and rarely argued about calls.

I positioned my feet at the line, wiped my palms on my shorts, and readied myself to shoot. As the official handed me the ball I heard one of our opponents lined up at the free throw lane protest to the official.

"Hey, she wasn't the one that was fouled!" she said, pointing to me.

The official ignored her plea as I sank both free throws to win the game. Kathy and I laughed at our little plot as we jogged off the court toward the locker room. None of the coaches or bench officials had noticed the mix-up.

During the drive back to campus I began feeling remorseful. In the heat of the battle I had let my competitiveness to win at all costs overrule honesty and integrity. That was the first time I had cheated in a sport, and I was embarrassed at my behavior. I had flunked the *sports-helps-you-develop-character test* that night. I vowed that I would never let that happen again.

*****

One evening I was alone in my room studying for a physiology exam when one of my sorority sisters bounded into the room. Jane was a year ahead of me in school. She had long blonde hair that was perfectly straight and cascaded down to the middle of her back. As a pledge in the sorority I had memorized various facts about each of the upperclassman, so I knew that Jane was from Indianapolis and a political science major. She was very bright and articulate to the point that during rush she was always assigned to the recruits that we really wanted in our house. She had an easy-going style and was a great conversationalist on any topic.

Jane plopped down on an overstuffed chair and pulled out a notebook. "Debbie, do you have a few minutes?"

"Sure, Jane, what's up?" I leaned back in my chair and closed my physiology textbook. "I'm always looking for an excuse to concentrate on something other than the ATP metabolism cycle."

"For my journalism class tomorrow I have to interview someone and turn in the notes from the interview. I thought since you are the star of the women's basketball team I would interview you."

"I'm flattered! Ask away," I responded.

Jane proceeded to ask probing questions about the challenges of being a female student-athlete. She explored my feelings about gender inequities, social and cultural issues, and the delicate balance of competitiveness and femininity. I enjoyed our conversation which eventually transpired into her sharing with me her dreams of working in the world of politics or journalism.

"I imagine it will be a tough go for you. I sure don't see many female reporters and, of course, there are zero women news anchors," I sighed.

"Yeah, but like you, we women are blazing a new trail," she added with a broad smile. She glanced at her watch. "Hey, gotta go. Thanks for the interview."

She scooped up her notebook and pencils and scurried out of my room. I leaned out into the hallway and shouted at her as she was walking down the hall.

"Just the first of many interviews I'm sure you'll be doing in your life, Jane Pauley!" I shouted to her. She turned and grinned while waving her hand with a "thumbs up" into the air.

*****

The American Association for Health, Physical Education and Recreation (AAHPER) was a national educational organization of elementary, secondary, and college physical education and health teachers. Within AAHPER a new commission was formed. This new commission was composed of women physical educators from colleges across the country. Called the Commission on Intercollegiate Athletics for Women (CIAW), this group was directed to organize and sponsor national sports championships for college women. Coach Mehnert informed our team that the 1971 CIAW basketball championship would be "by invitation only." This was exciting news, and gave us new drive and purpose in our competitions.

We proceeded to win the Indiana and Midwest collegiate tournaments. Our record was 16-1 when we received an invitation to play in the CIAW national finals. Sixteen teams from across the country would be headed to Western Carolina University the last week of March to vie for the championship. We excitedly packed our bags and piled into a van for the eight-hour drive to Cullowhee, North Carolina. As we approached the Smoky Mountains, we encountered a rare spring snowstorm. Coach Mehnert maintained a steel grip on the steering wheel as we crawled along the interstate amidst the blowing, swirling snow. We players kept quiet as the snow began falling more heavily, making vision difficult in the mountain passes and steep inclines. Whereas we should have arrived in Cullowhee by late afternoon, nightfall was upon us as Coach Mehnert drove slowly through the deepening snow. We felt sorry for Coach, whose face and body displayed the tension of her task. As the night wore on, we took turns staying awake to keep Coach Mehnert focused and alert. We stopped periodically to clear the windshield wipers of caked ice and snow. Our eight-hour drive turned into a fifteen-hour agonizing journey. After arriving and grabbing a few hours sleep in a Western Carolina University dormitory, we played our first game early the next morning, beating Winthrop College, 66-49. In our second game, we met a superior team, West Chester State, and lost 72-44. After watching Mississippi State College defeat West Chester State in the championship game, they announced the All-tournament Team. I was the only Indiana University player selected. Our first exposure to national competition was completed, and my sophomore basketball season was finished. A weary Coach Mehnert drove us back to Bloomington.

*****

On a whim I tried out for the women's fast pitch softball team in the spring, and made the final cut. It was fun meeting a new group of female athletes and getting my competitive juices flowing in a different sport. I played third base. Since there was no money for each sport to have its own uniforms, the softball team wore the basketball uniforms once the basketball season was over. The volleyball inherited these same uniforms in the fall.

It was great to be outdoors and enjoy the fragrances and warm sunshine of the Indiana spring. We played many of the same schools that we had played in basketball. During our final softball game at Ball State University I was used as a pinch hitter. We were down 2-1 in the last inning with two outs and a runner on second base. The coach called on me to bat. As I carefully dug my feet into position in the batter's box and took a few practice swings, I heard the umpire behind the plate speak with a detectable tone of sarcasm. "Look, it's Dead-Eye Debbie here to win the game!"

I stepped out of the batter's box and glared at the umpire. I didn't know who she was or how she knew my nickname. She pulled up her mask and grinned at me. It was Ball State's women's basketball coach! I nodded to her and returned a weak smile even though her comment disturbed me. Was she mocking me or speaking out of respect?

In this fledgling environment of women's sports, it was commonplace to have home teams supply the officials. There was barely enough money to support a team, let alone pay referees and umpires. Additionally, there were few trained women officials. My prediction was that the field of officiating would expand along with the women's sports movement. It was only a matter of time. In the meantime, this circumstance gave true meaning to the phrase "home court advantage."

I stepped back into the batter's box and refocused on my task of getting a base hit. Unfortunately Dead-Eye

Debbie did not win the game as I pounded an easily caught ball into the outfield for the final out. As I trotted back to our dugout, the players in the opposing dugout chanted, "**Dead-Eye Debbie** ... **Dead-Eye Debbie**." It took all of my inner strength to look straight ahead and not shout back or show them a rude gesture. I tried to rationalize that they were chanting out of respect for me as their basketball opponent, but I wasn't 100 percent convinced. The game, softball season, and my sophomore year were over.

CHAPTER 9

LESSONS IN LOSS, LIFE, AND LOVE

It seemed an injustice that my high school years seemed to drag, yet my college years were flying by so quickly. By my junior year our basketball team had sustained its reputation as one of the best teams in the Midwest. My teammates and I relished our lofty status in the emerging women's collegiate basketball world. Because of our successes, we now had a reporter from the campus newspaper assigned to us. We also had a new coach. Irene Mehnert had completed her studies and moved away. Our new coach, Bea Gorton, was a young graduate student working on a doctorate in kinesiology. She had played basketball at Wheaton College. Even though Coach Gorton was small in stature and had a quiet, subdued personality, she shared our passion for the game and often scrimmaged with us. Coach Gorton informed us that the CIAW had been replaced by a new national organization called the Association for Intercollegiate Athletics for Women

(AIAW). The AIAW was a more sophisticated governing body for women's collegiate sports that was organizing its first national basketball championship with strict regional qualifying tournaments. The first *official* women's national collegiate champion would be crowned in March! This gave us an incentive to keep working hard. In addition, we had some new girls on the team who were talented and possessed the same competitive fire that I had. We were excited.

Now that many colleges and universities had women's basketball teams, I noticed an odd difference between the men's and women's teams across the country. Men's teams had many African-American players, whereas I saw only a few black females playing on basketball teams. We had one African-American teammate, and she was on the junior varsity team. Yvonne was a jovial spirit. She was talkative and constantly telling funny stories. Jokingly we informed her that she was our "token black," and she got a charge out of being the center of attention. In fact, she told us to call her "Buckwheat," which I personally viewed as a degrading nickname, but she seemed to relish it. One time when she and I were alone I asked Buckwheat why more black girls didn't play basketball. She told me that it was strictly cultural.

"Black brothers don't like their women playing sports," she explained. I told her that it was a shame because I knew there had to be some very good black female athletes who were missing their calling. As much as black men were dominating men's basketball, I assumed black women would eventually do the same in the women's game once cultural norms changed. After all, we white girls hadn't been welcomed with open arms by our white brothers! I envisioned a slow evolution of acceptance would eventually occur in the African-American circles in the years to come.

*****

One of the benefits of being in a sorority was interaction with fraternities. I hadn't dated a lot in high school, so I enjoyed this social scene. There were fun parties and dances. During my first two years I dated several different fraternity guys. With three brothers and many childhood "boy buddies," I was comfortable around guys. But I soon discovered in the dating world that guys do not want to be beaten in anything by a female. On group dates that included any type of sport like bowling, Ping Pong, or billiards, my dates were not happy that I was better than them, or worse yet, would *beat* them. In fact, most of my female friends and sorority sisters appeared weak (or at least pretended to be) around their boyfriends. Even though most guys loved to talk about sports, I learned that they are only interested in *men's* sports. My dates were always impressed with my knowledge about various athletes and teams, and we would have lively conversations about current sporting events. They liked a girl who could talk sports and knew what was going on when we watched games together. But it ended there. Few were interested in my status as an accomplished athlete or the successes of the women's basketball team. Whereas most college girls thrived on the prestige of dating a male athlete, guys did not typically pursue dates with female athletes.

Being a female athlete meant dealing with a lot of mixed messages. I wanted to be feminine and attractive to men, but I couldn't cover up my competitive nature. A lot of men say they like independent women, but when it comes down to it they don't. A female's dependence is another person's power and control. As discouraging as it was for me, I refused to lower myself to appear weak or subservient. I had to be myself. I was attracted to several men, but was struggling to find one who appreciated and respected me for being both a female *and* an athlete.

One evening after one of my regular pick-up basketball games at the gym, one of the guys I was playing with asked me to join him for a Coke after the game. Greg Stokes was an outfielder on the varsity baseball team. He was smart, polite, athletic, and respected me for my athletic skills. He had short, wavy blonde hair and adorable dimples when he smiled. Greg and I clicked. We began studying together on week nights and going out on weekends. He didn't care that I played hard against him in pick-up basketball games and got sweaty. He didn't mind that I could beat him at bowling and tennis. He never jumped for joy at my winning, but since he had a sister who was athletic, he told me that he understood me---as long as I would still kiss him and hold his hand.

Greg became my special date for sorority social events. He came to my basketball games and I attended his baseball games. We became a steady couple. I invited Greg to go home with me over Christmas Break to meet my family. He blended in well with my brothers, and my parents adored him. I had a new drawer in my life---a serious boyfriend.

*****

As much as I appreciated the opportunity to play a sport in college, I was discouraged at the obvious inequities that existed between men's and women's sports. The basketball players on the men's team had athletic scholarships that paid their tuition, room and board. They traveled by luxury buses or airplanes, had practice and game uniforms laundered for them, and an endless supply of free shoes. Accommodations and food on the road were first-class. They practiced and played their games in a huge arena. They had multiple coaches, a training staff, and a wide array of special campus services. Even though we women had a better win-loss record than the men, we had to scrape for travel, food, and uniform money. We played our games in a dusty, dimly-lit gymnasium that had no bleachers. It seemed so unfair. We worked just as hard as the men and were representing the university in stellar fashion around the Midwest. By February we had a twelve-game winning streak going.

A few of the large regional newspapers wrote stories about our team, but it was annoying to have the articles appear on the "women's" pages or lifestyle section rather than in the sports section. In one article I was referred to as **"the blue-eyed cutie whose jump shot accuracy will amaze you if you can take your eyes off that beautiful form floating into the air."** I found this phrasing offensive and degrading.

"She sure doesn't shoot like a girl," one male reporter wrote. *Like a girl?* I thought as I read the article. *I shoot a jump shot the way it's supposed to be shot---male or female.*

Even though I liked the publicity, I was disgusted that we weren't treated with the same seriousness as male athletes. There was a slant of sexism in every article. **"Come out and watch the prettiest athletes on campus battle the Purdue coeds on the hard court. Check out this attractive winning crew,"** the newspaper reported. *Why can't we be appreciated for our beautiful jump shots and pretty behind-the-back passes?* I thought.

My consternation reached the boiling point when our team was invited to a two-day tournament in Illinois and we were told by Coach Gorton to bring a sleeping bag, pillow, and extra money. Apparently our accommodations were to be a classroom where we would be sleeping on the floor. Meals would be trips to a grocery store. Upon returning from that trip my teammate, Pat Archer, and I collaborated on a letter to the president of Indiana University, complaining about the second-class status we received from the university as female athletes. We mailed a copy of our letter to the Indiana University Foundation, an organization that manages private donations and conducts fund-raising campaigns to support extra needs at the university. Within a week our action resulted in my first lesson in diplomacy.

"Debbie Millbern and Pat Archer," our kinesiology professor announced in class, "Dean Aldrich wants to see you both in her office immediately after class."

As Pat and I approached the dean's office, I thought to myself, *Good! Maybe things will change.*

Dr. Anita Aldrich was the head of the women's physical education department. After seeing her, I guessed that she had arrived on campus during the

Conestoga wagon days. Her hair was snow-white and pulled back into a tight bun. Her small pearl earrings sank into her large, fleshy earlobes. Her face was etched with deep wrinkles and her flowered polyester dress was cinched loosely at the waist with a narrow black belt. She peered at Pat and me over her bifocals from behind a massive oak desk as her secretary ushered us into the office.

We sat down in stiff, leather chairs across from Dean Aldrich. I noticed that most of her office walls were adorned with elegantly framed certificates with fancy calligraphy and large embossed seals. I didn't see any sports pictures or trophies in the room. My feeling of exhilaration and triumph was slowly dissipating as I surveyed the scene. My intuition said that this was not going to be a happy meeting.

"I received a call yesterday from the president," Dean Aldrich said in a slow, drawling voice that reminded me of Count Dracula. She stared at Pat, then me, then cleared her throat. "I understand that you wrote to him with your concerns about the treatment of women athletes."

Pat and I glanced at each other. After a few moments of nervous silence I replied, "Absolutely. I don't think it's fair that the guys get so much and we receive so little. We just went to a two-day tournament, which we won, by the way, and we had to sleep on the floor in a classroom!"

I was trying desperately to steady the quiver in my voice, but didn't mind emitting a slight tone of agitation. Pat nodded her head enthusiastically in a display of solidarity and comradeship.

Dean Aldrich sat up straighter and leaned forward with her forearms delicately placed on her desk. "Do you know what is meant by 'chain of command'?" she asked snidely. Her eyes registered betrayal.

"Not really," Pat and I answered simultaneously. I wondered where she was going with this question.

"A chain of command is the hierarchy of officials through which an action is taken," she stated. Her verbiage and intonation made it sound as if she were reading a definition from a dictionary. I stared at her and felt my face begin to flush and my armpits sweat. She continued. "And you *both* failed to follow that chain of command by writing directly to the president rather than starting with me. I am very upset that you would go over my head like that," she said, concealing her rancor with a smirk.

Troubling thoughts whirled through my head. *Uh oh. This is not good.*

"Furthermore, you must realize that change takes time. You women are playing for fun, not rewards or entitlements. So, appreciate what you have and the opportunity that you have been given."

I know I should have felt like a spoiled brat, but I didn't. I wanted to argue that Susan B. Anthony and Rosa Parks had fought for equality without regard for this so-called "chain of command." They fought for a right. I remained silent and looked down at my shoes, afraid to make eye contact with Pat. I decided to cut my losses and not dig a deeper hole for myself, but it was my perception that Dean Aldrich was more upset about our lack of following the rules, rather than the insult of the inequalities we had presented. Trying desperately to mask the irritation in my voice, I responded with a weak, "I'm sorry," even though I wasn't the least bit so. Pat squeaked out a "me too."

We left the Dean's office and walked in silence to basketball practice. The shock and embarrassment of what we had just experienced was numbing. The slush of the melting snow on the sidewalk seeped over the top of my loafers, soaking my socks. My spirit was equally soaked. *When will women athletes begin earning respect?* I thought. *Will we ever get equal treatment?*

My mind became less troubled as I reached the gymnasium and slipped into my basketball sneakers. I picked up a basketball and dribbled down the court as fast as I could, lofting a fifteen-foot jump shot into the air. As it fell flawlessly through the net, I smiled. *Oh what a glorious feeling*, I thought, sensing my frustrations evaporating for the moment. Moving my body around the court transformed my mind into a state of exhilaration. Like a drug, playing this game numbed my brain with incalculable pleasure. *Maybe this purest of feelings is what sports are meant to be about*, I thought. I executed a series of zig-zag dribbles down the court and continued my musings. My supposition was that change was probably on its way, and Dean Aldrich was most likely treading slowly in the male-dominated world of sports competition. Because of my youthful exuberance, however, I was growing impatient. *Maybe I am being ungrateful, but I sure don't think it's fair that my teammates and I have to make our own ham sandwiches to eat in a restroom before a game,* I thought, as I tossed up a free throw and watched the ball softly kiss the front of the rim and snap the white net cords as it fell through the net. Pat and I never heard back from the Indiana University Foundation.

*****

"Welcome to the first AIAW Collegiate National Basketball Championship," the announcer shouted over the intercom. The players paraded in formation into the Illinois State University arena wearing their team uniforms. The greens, blues, reds, purples, and yellows created a colorful collage across the gymnasium floor. My teammates and I stood proudly at attention as all sixteen participating teams from across the country were announced. The referees stood in a line facing us. Wearing their black- and white-striped shirts, they looked like a perfectly aligned row of zebras. The flash of cameras filled the arena. My heart was pounding and my stomach felt like there was already a miniature basketball game being played inside it. We had earned our place in the national tournament after winning our regional tournament.

It was interesting that the best women's college basketball teams in the country were not necessarily from the largest universities. We could handily beat Notre Dame, yet struggled against Franklin College. Duke might get beat by Winthrop College, and Ohio State could lose to Cedarville College. Since there were no athletic scholarships or enticements for female athletes, a small college in New York might be blessed with enough good players to beat the University of Connecticut. As a result, several of the schools who qualified for the AIAW Nationals were small and relatively unknown. Even though Indiana University was a large, well-known school, our budget for women's basketball was no larger than that for a small school. All women's teams struggled for the most basic financial resources.

After the opening ceremony concluded, we played our first game of the tournament, defeating Southern Connecticut State by a score of 49-30. We were on our way! The next day we met our match against a small Catholic college called Immaculata. Made up primarily of girls who grew up playing basketball in the Catholic prep schools of Philadelphia, the Immaculata girls were big and aggressive. Even though their uniforms consisted of pale blue tunic skirts worn over white blouses, their style of play was far from ladylike. They played extremely rough and, at times, even dirty. We weren't used to such physicality and, even though we battled hard, came up short, 46-43. Their fan base was a bleacherful of nuns banging on pots and pans. We were devastated to see our season end with such a tough loss. I felt unfulfilled.

As we sat in the bleachers the next day and watched Immaculata defeat West Chester State to win the national championship, my teammates and I vowed that we would be back next year, tougher and stronger. I kiddingly told them that maybe we could find some nuns with pots and pans to cheer for us. Everyone laughed and promised to work harder individually over the summer. We understood what it would take to win.

"Thank God we don't have to wear ugly tunics like they do!" one of my teammates exclaimed, prompting more laughter.

Playing against national champions Immaculata

As we were leaving the arena a college-age woman approached me. She was dressed in street clothes and had her long chestnut brown hair pulled back into a pony tail. She grabbed my arm and pulled me aside. She had brown piercing eyes that stared directly into my eyes. My teammates stopped and gathered around her.

"Hi," she said with a slight grin on her face. "My name is Tara VanDerveer and I am going to transfer to your school next year."

I was perplexed, and asked, "Really? Where are you from?"

"I play basketball at the University of Albany, in New York. I came out here to watch this entire tournament, and I really love the way your team plays. You play with such great finesse and teamwork, so I want to be on your team next season."

"That would be great," I said, thinking to myself, *who is this girl?* "Have you ever been to Indiana?" I asked.

"Nope, but I'll see you there next year."

Tara reached out to shake my hand, and then turned abruptly to walk away. She walked with a stride of confidence and her head held high.

"Now that's gutsy," I said to my teammates as we started walking toward our van.

*****

"Debbie, I love you and want to marry you."

While sitting on the patio of the Kappa house, Greg Stokes spoke these words to me as we held hands. Spring loveliness had permeated every fragment of campus and only a few weeks of school remained. Greg would be graduating and moving to Chicago to begin working on his MBA in the fall. I still had my senior year ahead of me at Indiana.

"Transfer to the University of Chicago so that we can be together," he pleaded.

I hesitated before I spoke. His soft brown eyes showed an eagerness that made my heart ache.

"Greg, I am so honored that you want to marry me." I choked a little as I continued. "But I have my final year of college and basketball ahead of me. I don't want to get married or transfer schools."

Greg's face drained of color and tears began to well in his eyes. "Do you mean that you love basketball more than me?" His voice was hushed, laced with anxiety.

I looked down at our intertwined fingers and brought my other hand to cup his hand in both of mine.

"Greg, I can't marry you." I paused. "I'm not in love with you."

Greg pulled his hand from my grip and stood. His demeanor changed abruptly from sweetness to agitation. His face became flushed.

"You can't mean that," he stammered. "I can't believe that you'd choose basketball over me."

It wasn't so much that I was *choosing* between Greg and basketball, as far as I was concerned. Marriage is serious business. When I was sixteen my grandfather told me that the two most important decisions made in life are: one's career choice; and one's marriage partner. And, he noted that if either of those decisions is wrong, it will ruin the other. I had a pretty good idea on my career choice, but my life partner was unfortunately not on my radar screen yet.

"I'm sorry, but I can't," I said as I began to cry. "I have to follow my heart."

Greg turned from me and walked swiftly down the steps. He turned and looked back at me and then began running across the lawn, disappearing behind the science building. Greg ran out of my life as I sat in turmoil. I sat for awhile and listened to the birds chirping loudly in the large magnolia trees near the patio. The lilacs filled the air with a sweet aroma, but there was no sweetness in my spirit. My stomach ached and I suddenly felt light-headed. *What have I done?* I thought.

That evening I called my parents to tell them what had happened. I was desperate for reassurance and support for my decision. I rambled on about how Greg was a great guy and a wonderful friend, but I didn't love him and couldn't give up my final basketball season to be with him. My mother simply stated that she was sorry to hear it. My dad talked more, but his final statement was like a dagger into my gut.

"Debbie," he said, "I doubt if you'll ever find a guy as perfect as Greg Stokes. You may have made the biggest mistake in your life."

I sobbed as I said good-bye and hung up the phone. I sat alone in my room listening to some sorority sisters down the hall singing along with a Carole King album playing on their record player.

"It's too late, baby, now it's too late; though we really did try to make it. Something inside has died and I can't hide and I just can't fake it."

Even though Greg is considered a "great catch," I can't fake it, I said to myself. I wasn't yet panicky over finding Mr. Right, and was hopeful that I hadn't bought an admission ticket to the sisterhood of spinsters.

I didn't attend Greg's graduation ceremony, nor did I ever hear from him again.

CHAPTER 10

SENIOR YEAR UPS AND DOWNS

As I drove toward campus in August of 1972, I was experiencing a myriad of emotions. This would be my last fall, winter, and spring for many things--- college classes, basketball, and sorority. I would be student teaching in the spring, then graduating and searching for a job. The college chapter of my life was going to end, and the umbilical cord with dear friends and teammates would be cut. My four years at Indiana University would be the longest that I had lived in one place my entire life. It had been my first opportunity to develop solid, enduring friendships and I was saddened by the thought of it ending.

I had spent the summer recovering from the emotional severance from Greg and felt comfortable with my decision, even though I sensed my parents' fear of my becoming an old maid. I was eager to concentrate on making this final basketball season the best one yet. A husband could come later, I figured. At least I hoped so.

After settling into my room and greeting several of my sorority sisters, I headed to the gymnasium. Even though I had practiced a lot over the summer, I was excited to pound the hardwood on my glorious campus again. Alone in the gym, I dribbled and began shooting. The staccato rhythm of the ball hitting the floor was mesmerizing as I lost myself in my beloved game. After several shots I stopped and gripped the basketball tightly in both hands. Walking to the center of the court, I sat down cross-legged within the center circle and hugged the ball against my chest. The wonderful scent of leather filled my nostrils. The smell of possibilities surrounded me. I bowed my head, placing my forehead on the ball, and said a silent prayer: "*God, you gave me athletic talent and a competitive nature. Thank you for fulfilling my prayer of getting to play on a real basketball team. Please let good things happen to me this final season. Help me absorb, appreciate, and remember every second of every game. I don't want to forget one single moment, because I know this will be the final season for me.*"

I turned my head so that my cheek rested on the ball, and I looked up at the braided white net hanging from the bright orange basketball rim. This love affair with basketball had grown from my early years on a driveway court to a full-blown passion. I had an overwhelming feeling of happiness and contentment. This was going to be a great year.

*****

Over the summer a new law had been passed by the federal government. Called Title IX, it was actually a part of the 1972 Equal Opportunity in Education Act. Title IX evolved from complaints about discrimination on the basis of sex in hiring and employment. Whereas women's rights issues had lost momentum after the suffrage movement in the early 1900s, feminist activities re-emerged with the passing of the Civil Rights Act of 1964. Many women across the country had been filing formal complaints citing inequities in pay, rank, admissions, and treatment at various universities. The founding of the National Organization for Women (NOW) in 1966 accelerated lobbying action. Thus, Title IX became law on June 23, 1972. It stated that *"No person in the United States shall, on the basis of sex, be excluded from participation in, denied the benefits of, or be subjected to discrimination under any education program or activity receiving Federal assistance."*

There was no mention of athletics in the law, but since all high schools and colleges receive federal funding for athletic programs, there was talk about how the scenery was about to change for women athletes. Equal opportunity was on the horizon. Some male journalists condemned the law and predicted that Title IX would ruin men's sports. **"There is only so much money to go around,"** one sports reporter wrote. **"No one wants to spend money to watch women play,"** he continued.

"What about the educational benefits derived from playing a sport---male *or* female," I shouted as I tossed the newspaper onto the table. "Why don't they write about that?"

My hope for instant equality faded once I learned that schools were given several years to comply with the new law. As an athlete I was disappointed that I would not get to personally experience the full ramifications of Title IX. Equality was on its way, but it would be beneficial to future female athletes rather than to me. Nevertheless, for my senior season our basketball team was getting new uniforms. In the past, we never had warm-up outfits, so warm-ups were ordered for us. Even though they were navy blue (and our school colors were cream and crimson), we were happy that we didn't have to provide our own miscellaneous jackets and pants, AND we would look like a real team. I later found out that the warm-ups were a special inexpensive, close-out purchase---and navy blue was the only color available. Unlike the men, we still had to launder our own uniforms, however, and pay for our own sneakers. We got some meal money, even though we still traveled in a van driven by Coach Gorton. When we had to stay overnight, we were provided a hotel room, with four players assigned to a room. The men stayed two to a room. The most exciting change was getting to play some of our home games in the brand new Assembly Hall, a huge arena where the men played their games. However, we still had to practice in a small auxiliary gym, which dissipated any home court advantage. Things were beginning to change, just not fast enough for me. There were still no scholarships, letter jackets, full-time coaches, training tables, weight-rooms, training rooms, or other campus services. We still didn't have a team locker room. All of the women athletes shared the common locker room with the female physical education majors along with all of the women on campus. And, our competition schedule was only seventeen games, compared to over thirty for the men.

*****

As I walked into the gymnasium the first day of basketball practice, there she was---Tara VanDerveer--- the girl who had talked to us the previous March at the AIAW National Championship. She had done exactly what she promised and had transferred to Indiana University! I jogged over to greet her and welcome her to the team. I watched her warm up and shoot. She was purposeful in her preparation and had a serious demeanor about her. I could tell that she was going to be a great addition to our team. I had a tingling feeling that this might be *our* year.

We started the season with two big wins. I was the captain and the only senior in our starting line up. Debbie Oing, Carol Kegley, Jorja Hoehn, Tara VanDerveer, and I gelled quickly as a starting unit. And we had a strong sixth player in Pat Archer, who had been a starter the previous year. We were fearless, and had become accustomed to Coach Gorton's easy-going coaching style. She was soft-spoken, and rarely raised her voice. She realized that she was coaching a group of players who knew the game, and she was a masterful conductor of a symphony of good athletes.

Our first home contest in the Assembly Hall arena was amazing. Suspended from the ceiling were the huge red NCAA championship banners won by the men's team. The upholstered theater-style seats seemed to extend to the heavens. The bright lights made the rims the brightest hue of orange I had ever seen and the shiny hardwood floor seemed to have some extra "give" to it, making it easier to run and jump. Instead of a hard bench, there were red padded chairs for us to sit on. *Indiana University* was printed on the back cushion of each chair. I wished we could practice every day in this spectacular arena instead of merely playing a few home games in it.

As we were shooting around two hours before the game, Bob Knight, the men's basketball coach, stepped onto the court. He was wearing khaki pants and a red sweater with "Indiana Basketball" stitched on the front in white cursive lettering. As he wandered over toward the sideline, he waved to our coach and then leaned casually against the scorer's table watching us warm up.

"How many points you gonna get tonight, Millbern?" he shouted to me in his normal gruff voice.

I grinned. "As many as I can, Coach." I respected Coach Knight and was excited that he took an interest in our team. He had spent several sessions advising Coach Gorton on specific offensive and defensive strategies.

"I wish I could get some of my guys to play as hard and confident as you gals play," Coach Knight responded.

I nodded to him and continued to shoot my jump shots. "We hope to add some banners of our own in here, Coach," I replied as I snagged a rebounded shot.

Approximately four hundred spectators attended this first-ever women's game in the Assembly Hall. Even though the crowd seemed sparse in the 17,000-seat arena, it didn't diminish the overwhelming thrill that our team felt. There was no pep band or cheerleaders or the singing of the *Star Spangled Banner*, but it was a big step for our women's program to have the opportunity to play in a big-time venue. We won the game 54-46 against Indiana State University.

For our third game of the season we traveled to Illinois State University, the site of the previous year's national championship. We were eager to play a good game since our last outing there resulted in our bitter, final defeat of the season. We were playing well and were leading at halftime. During the second half while coming down with a rebound, I landed on another player's foot. My ankle had been tightly taped so it did not twist. Instead, I heard a pop in my left knee. The pain was excruciating as I collapsed to the ground. The referee whistled a dead ball as I clutched my knee. I had never felt such intense pain in my life. The crowd was hushed as my teammates carried my off the court. Our undergraduate student trainer immediately applied an ice bag to my knee. I could tell that my injury was serious because I couldn't put any weight on my left leg without agonizing pain. I sat in a blind stupor watching the remainder of the game with my leg propped up on the bleacher. We won the game by five points, and my teammates showered and changed while I stayed in my warm-ups for the long drive back to Bloomington. My knee hurt so bad that I was nauseous for most of the drive home. The trainer wrapped my knee and gave me crutches to use. One of my teammates drove me to the sorority house where I limped to bed and cried myself to sleep. Even though my leg was elevated on two pillows, it throbbed all night. Every time I moved, I awoke in pain.

Because women athletes did not have access to team physicians or other professional athletic trainers, I spent several days icing, elevating, and wrapping my knee on my own. I stayed on crutches for two weeks, camped in the bleachers watching our practices and games. Our super-sub, Pat Archer, took my place in the starting line-up. My physical pain was matched equally by my mental pain as I watched my senior season slowly slipping away. When I was finally able to walk gingerly on it, the student trainer wrapped my knee very tightly so that I could at least shoot around at practice. I was determined to play again and finally did so after watching our team suffer its first loss of the season by one point. I had missed five games.

My knee was wrapped so tightly that I could barely feel my foot as I jogged down the court. It hurt and felt unstable, but I continued to play. I was less effective as a player since it was difficult for me to push off and make hard cuts. My signature move was to fake hard in one direction, then cut around a screen set by a teammate and drain a jump shot. Now, however, I couldn't jump as high and wasn't as quick. My body would not respond to my commands. My teammates and coach encouraged me to keep playing as long as I could endure it. It was discouraging to lack the precision and strength on which I had thrived.

The season progressed and even though my point production had dropped, we were 14-1 as we entered the qualifying regional tournament held in Cedarville, Ohio. At the regionals, we were housed in a college dormitory. Tara VanDerveer and I shared a small room with a bunk bed. It had a bare linoleum floor and a single window that wouldn't close all of the way. With Tara lying in the top bunk and me in the bottom, we talked late into the night about our love for basketball and our shared dream of being national champions.

"Do you suppose women will ever earn scholarships to play basketball in college?" I asked her.

"Maybe someday. But it's probably too late for us," she answered.

I pulled the blanket tightly to my chin to keep out the chill. "It sure would've been nice to at least earn *something*," I sighed. "The guys are so lucky."

I closed my eyes and thought back to my prayer as a little girl for God to transform me overnight into a boy so that I could play on a team. I turned onto my right side and slipped a pillow under my aching knee. With the March wind whistling through the window I drifted to sleep and dreamed of making a game-winning shot at the national finals.

As they had all season, my teammates did a good job of picking up for my scoring slack, and we beat Michigan State and Ohio State in the regional championship to earn our second trip to the national finals.

The second AIAW National Tournament was being held at Queens College in New York City, and for the first time, we weren't going to travel the long distance in a van. Coach Gorton announced in practice that the Indiana University Foundation was graciously providing us their private plane. Upon hearing her announcement, our team began to hoot and holler. Pat Archer and I looked at each other with broad, satisfying grins. Maybe our letter to the Foundation a year earlier *had* made a difference! Once again, most of the sixteen teams at the nationals were not big-name schools. There was no Stanford, Tennessee, or Notre Dame. Without the lure of athletic scholarships, the women's basketball powerhouses continued to be schools like Immaculata College, Queens College, Mercer College, and Stephen Austin College.

Though they were both close and hard-fought, we won our first two games against Lehman College and East Stroudsburg State. That placed us into the Final Four. We were only two games short of our goal! Next for us was a game against the host school, Queens College. Last year's champion, Immaculata College, was playing Southern Connecticut in the other semi-final. Unfortunately the schedule required us to play our semi-final game the same evening as our afternoon quarter-final game against East Stroudsburg. Therefore, we only had four hours rest between contests. Because our hotel was a considerable distance from the gym, we went downstairs to the empty cafeteria, turned out the lights, and laid on the tables and cold linoleum floor to rest. Our manager took our uniforms to a nearby Laundromat to wash. Coach Gorton left to buy sandwiches, fruit, and water for our dinner. It was impossible to sleep because our adrenalin levels were so high, but it felt good to rest. With only small streaks of light filtering through the cracks of the steel cafeteria door, we talked softly in the dim light about our dreams to win it all.

Playing so many games in such a short time span was taking its toll on my knee. Just like last year's tournament, sixteen teams were battling over four intense days to win a national championship. By now my knee ached with every step, but I was determined to gut it out. There would not be another national tournament for me.

The Queens College game was a nightmare. My legs felt tired and my knee throbbed. Without leg power, my shooting was off. The rest of the team struggled as well. I dug in and played as hard as I could, diving for balls, jumping for rebounds, taking charges, and playing aggressive defense. We got out of sync and our stamina faded. I felt like I was playing in slow motion. The Queens team had a deeper bench and had not been forced to play three games within a twenty-four-hour span as we had. They wore us down. When the final buzzer sounded we had lost by twelve points.

I was devastated as the reality of playing my final game and losing engulfed me. My basketball career had come to a sorrowful end, one game short of playing for a national championship. After shaking hands with the opposing team, I limped to the locker room and sat at the end of the bench, listening to Coach Gorton rave about our courage and selflessness as a team. I sat in a stupor as she talked about *"pride," "representing Indiana University," "lessons learned,"* and *"character."* She ended by talking about *"next season."* I was numb to her words. All I could think about was the sport that I adored more than anything in the world was over for me.

As the team dispersed to begin showering and changing, I slowly began stripping the heavy bandage off of my knee. The pain in my knee pulsated as I pulled off each strand of sweat-soaked gauze. My socks were bloody as I peeled them from my feet.

Large blood blisters covered the bottoms of both feet. I suddenly felt an arm around my shoulder. Coach Gorton sat down and leaned close to my face.

"Debbie, you gave it your all," she whispered into my ear. "You were an inspiration to all of us this season, and we'll never forget it." We sat together in silence broken only by the distant echo of banging pots and pans by the Immaculata nuns cheering on their team in the other semi-final game.

I wept as I became overcome with grief. I wept as I had never wept before. I sobbed unashamedly out of sheer heartbreak. Sweat was intermingled with tears as I cried into my jersey---the jersey that I would never wear again. I cried for that little girl who had wanted to play so badly and that bigger girl who had reached the end. I cried for having to say farewell to the one thing in my life that brought me the purest joy. The hours I had spent shooting baskets over the years had at times rescued me from loneliness and despair. It had filled holes in my life when I struggled to find my place. It had lifted me up with unconditional happiness. My tears were equally split between mourning our defeat and losing a portion of my heart.

The next day we watched Immaculata win its second AIAW championship over Queens College. Immaculata wore the same ugly tunics they had the previous year, and their nun cheerleaders still banged on pots and pans. As we left the gymnasium the star player on Immaculata's team approached me. "So long, good-lookin' with the eyes," she said as she trotted toward her team's bus.

On the long trip back to Indiana it was difficult to get the "what ifs" out of my mind. *What if* I hadn't hurt my knee this season? *What if* we hadn't been forced to play three games within twenty-four hours? Every athlete has a list of "what ifs" when they lose. In all fairness, though, in winning there are also "what ifs." *What if* I hadn't made that crucial free throw? *What if* I hadn't gotten away with that fifth foul? Sports are full of "what ifs." Life is full of "what ifs."

As we pulled into Bloomington, Coach Gorton announced that we were heading directly to the Assembly Hall arena. There was going to be a "welcome home" rally. The men's basketball team was getting into town just ahead of us from their NCAA Final Four where they had lost to UCLA in their semi-finals. Bob Knight had contacted our coach and invited the women's team to be included along with the men in the celebration. The Assembly Hall was packed with applauding fans as both teams paraded into the arena. Coach Knight and Coach Gorton hugged. Men and women basketball players hugged. A special bond of Hoosier competitiveness, school pride, and love for basketball permeated the gathering as both coaches spoke about their teams and introduced us individually to the crowd. It was an honorable gesture by Coach Knight to include us women. It was an event that remained fixed in my mind and was a temporary salve to my emotional wounds.

*****

As I completed my senior coursework and student teaching in the spring, the pain of losing at nationals merged with the agony of ending my overall college experience. I would be graduating and saying good-bye to so many things that contributed to my growth and development, and made me so happy. I would miss my sorority sisters, teammates, coaches, professors, and friends. I would miss the campus with its beautiful limestone buildings, fountains, and architectural features. This place felt like home, especially since this was the only time in my life I had spent four uninterrupted years living in one location. For once in my life I felt secure and that I belonged. The campus was a collage of color with redbuds, tulips, and forsythias in the spring. The sweet fragrance of lilacs filled my nostrils as I wandered around campus, past Beck Chapel and across the Jordan River. I wanted to drink in the landscape and imprint it permanently in my brain. My knee was finally healing, but still felt unstable at times. I hadn't touched a basketball since our final game at nationals.

Three weeks before graduating I received a phone call from my advisor. Dr. Norma Johnson was a physical education faculty member from whom I had taken several classes and met with twice every year to schedule each semester's coursework.

"Debbie, you've been selected to receive the Elvis J. Stahr Distinguished Senior Award," she said in a higher than normal pitch. The excitement was evident in her voice.

"The *what*?" I asked.

She continued. "Each year five outstanding seniors from the entire graduating class are awarded the Stahr Award based on excellence in academics and exceptional leadership and service to Indiana University. You're one of the five! It's the most prestigious award any senior can receive."

"Oh my gosh," I yelled into the phone. "How did *I* get selected?"

She didn't answer my question, but continued. "There'll be a banquet to honor the five awardees in two weeks. You should receive the formal invitation soon. And, your name will be permanently engraved on a plaque in the Memorial Union Building with all of the past winners. Congratulations, Debbie! Well done!"

The awards banquet was a fancy affair with white linen tablecloths, servers in formal attire, and fine food. The president of the university introduced each of us five recipients and read a summary of our accomplishments. Mom and Dad traveled from Columbus to attend. It was a proud occasion for us all. Dr. Norma Johnson sat at our table, and I learned that she had nominated me for the award with an extensive application that included support letters from a variety of professors, staff, and coaches at Indiana University.

My college experience was over. I graduated cum laude with a 3.89 grade point average and an 89 percent free-throw-shooting percentage. Both had taken a lot of work to achieve, but I was secretly more proud of my free throw percentage.

1973 IU Final Four Team at Queens College, New York

Front Row: Nancy Petrick (mgr), Kitty Unthank, Pat Archer,
Debbie Oing, Jane Christophersen, Evelyn Butler
Back Row: Bea Gorton (coach), Judy Bishop (asst. coach),
Margie Holland (trainer), Lou Stephenson, Donna Palivec,
Carol Kegley, Jorja Hoehn, Debbie Millbern, Tara VanDerveer

CHAPTER 11

THEY CALL ME COACH

"So, Miss Millbern, what sports can you coach?" Mr. Lemna asked. He continued, "With this Title IX thing, we're forced to expand our offerings you know."

Owen Lemna was the principal of Northside High School in Muncie, Indiana. It was July, 1973 and I was near the end of an interview for a position as one of the two new female physical education teachers. Mr. Lemna was a stout man with wavy salt-and-pepper hair. He had a warm smile, thick eyebrows, and over-sized ears. He was wearing a brightly colored plaid sports jacket and a navy blue and red striped tie. When he greeted me with a handshake his soft hands reminded me of my father's.

"What sports will you be offering for girls?" I asked.

"Well, first of all, I'll be honest. We really want you for the job, and definitely to be our girls' basketball coach. But you and the other PE teacher we hire this summer will have to coach *all* of the girls' sports---one sport each season." He pulled a pad of paper from his desk drawer and looked down at it, poised to write.

"So, in the fall would you prefer coaching volleyball or swimming?" he asked, still staring at his paper.

"Volleyball," I answered as I watched him write.

"Winter will be basketball, of course, so do you want track or tennis in the spring?"

After a moment of hesitation, I responded. "Tennis." Tennis would be less complicated, I guessed. Track has so many different events.

He wrote a few notes and put his pen down. "Great," he said. "Well, what do you think? Are you interested in the job?"

Northside High School was only a few years old. Its student population consisted mostly of upper middle-class white students. Many of their parents were professionals—doctors, nurses, teachers, attorneys, dentists, professors, bankers, and business owners. The small percentage of black students who attended the school were bused in from the east side of town. I enjoyed the tour of the building. It was immaculately clean and still had a scent of newness. Light green tiles lined the hallways, and the floors were so shiny that I had to squint from the glare as we walked past the huge glass entrance. The gymnasium had huge folding doors that separated into two smaller gyms---one for girls' classes and one for the boys. Like a smashed accordion, the bleachers were pushed high against the walls. My heart began racing as I peered into the gym, imagining that beautiful place as my own. A gigantic male Titan was painted on the concrete block wall. Standing with his hands on his hips, he conveyed an image of power and strength. The words *"This is Titan Country"* were printed in bold letters beneath his feet.

During the tour I met the secretaries and various staff. Everyone seemed friendly, and I liked Mr. Lemna. The salary was comparable to the other two positions where I had interviewed---$8,200 for the year.

"I accept the position, Mr. Lemna, and I look forward to teaching here," I told him when we settled back into his office.

"Terrific! We still have another gal to hire, and we'll give her the sports that you didn't choose to coach. That will be swimming, gymnastics, and track."

Mr. Lemna handed me a stack of papers as he stood. "Look these over. I'll be filling out the contract with the sports that you'll be coaching and getting it to you soon." I stood and gave him a firm handshake. He paused and then asked, "Oh, I just about forgot – cheerleaders or dance team?"

"What?" I asked politely.

"You have a choice to sponsor the cheerleaders or the dance team."

Voices echoed in my brain, the voices of all of the adults in my past who had suggested that I be a cheerleader rather than an athlete: *It is more acceptable. It is more feminine,*" they had all said. I still hated cheerleading!

"I'll gladly take the cheerleaders," I replied to Mr. Lemna, not believing what I had just said or how cheerful my tone had been.

Oh brother, I thought to myself. *This will be interesting. Three sports AND cheerleading!*

*****

When people say that teachers have it easy, they can't be referring to a first-year teacher. Or, for that matter, a second-year, fifth-year or even tenth-year teacher. I never worked so hard in my life. Thank goodness my apartment was only one block from the school, because I spent more time at school than in my apartment. I was teaching six periods of freshman girls' physical education, supervising cheerleading practice, and doing all of the tasks involved in coaching. Every morning I arrived at school before daybreak and dragged myself back to my apartment after dark. After preparing supper for myself I would plan the next day's lessons and team practice until my eyelids would not stay open. If my team had a game, I got home even later. At least I had the weekends to recover---except on the Friday and Saturday nights when the football team had a game. As cheerleading sponsor I was expected to attend all football games to supervise my cheerleaders. The biggest decisions with this group of gregarious girls focused around which skirt and sweater combination to wear and what hair ribbons and lipstick would match. I was helpless in contributing much to these decisions, but I kept reminding myself of something Mr. Lemna told me once I agreed to take on the cheerleaders.

"Make sure their skirts aren't too short and they don't look like sluts" he had said.

Actually, I found them to be a great group of girls who gave me little trouble. Their minor squabbles were easily resolved. I wasn't very helpful on suggestions for cheers and jumps since I had never been a cheerleader. Thank goodness they had attended cheerleading camp during the summer and mastered a large repertoire of cheers. I didn't mind attending the home football games, but having to ride the fan bus to away games with hormone-oozing high school students and cheerleaders was something I learned to dread.

One Friday in late September I hurried home after school to rest for a few hours before reporting back to school to catch the bus for a football game in Indianapolis. I plopped onto my sofa to rest. The combined emotional and physical fatigue I experienced in teaching and coaching exceeded anything I experienced as a college student and athlete. Back at Indiana University, I had been ready to party on Fridays. Now on Fridays all I wanted to do was sleep.

Soon after sitting down, my eyes closed and I began dreaming about a large yellow school bus floating on a cloud above a football field. The fans were cheering wildly as my cheerleaders waved from atop the bus. They were topless with ridiculously teased hair that extended to the heavens. My principal, Mr. Lemna, jumped from another cloud onto the bus and began honking the horn loudly in despair....Honk! Honk! Honk! The sound filled the air, drowning out the crowd. Suddenly I jerked awake.

Honk! Honk! Honk! There was that horn...a *real* horn! Shaking the fogginess from sleep, I jumped up from the sofa and ran to my window. I pulled back the drapes. It was dark outside. There on the street in front of my apartment was the fan bus, honking loudly for me. I heard my name shouted from the open windows. My cheerleaders were waving toward my apartment window.

"Miss Millbern! Come on!"

"Miss Millbern! Let's go!"

148

"Oh my gosh," I screamed. "I fell asleep and missed the bus!"

Thank goodness the bus driver knew where I lived. I grabbed my coat and dashed downstairs.

As the big bus door hissed open, the bus driver spoke. "I figured what had happened," he said with a smile. "Welcome aboard."

The students cheered loudly as I sheepishly waved to them and took my seat behind the driver. The big door slammed and off we went.

*****

I had no social life. Because of my hectic schedule there was no time for dating. Plus, my daily interaction with single men was nil. All of the male teachers with whom I worked were married. That was the bad news. The good news was that I was in love with my job. I was living my passion---teaching physical education and coaching. My day was filled with bells ringing in the hallways, squeaking tennis shoes on the gym floor, the smell of chili and pizza drifting into the gymnasium from the nearby cafeteria, and the chattering sounds of girls coming in and out of the locker room. I loved demonstrating tennis strokes, square dance steps, and soccer kicks. When my final class was finished at 3:15 each afternoon it seemed like all I wanted to do was lie down. But then the giggling voices of my athletes invading my office with talk of boyfriends or our next game at Yorktown sparked me to a new level of energy. My biggest challenge was finding time during the day to go to the bathroom.

Even though I mourned the end of my personal competitive career, and occasionally harbored still frames in my mind showing a frustrated, young girl sitting on the sidelines, I was thrilled to offer an opportunity that I never had---for high school girls to play on a team and compete for their school. I got a tremendous charge out of seeing young, adolescent "Debbies" looking to me for guidance. I still had a major competitive streak in my soul, so my mission was to transfer it to these budding athletes. I wanted these kids to feel my passion, drive, and enthusiasm for competing and winning. Oh, how I lamented that I had not been born six years later to have the opportunities that Title IX was providing for these girls.

Thankfully my competitive fire for basketball was partially fulfilled as I spent my lunch hour in the gymnasium playing basketball with the high school guys. I remembered how envious I had been of Mr. Barnes, my elementary gym teacher, who got to wear shorts for work. I not only wore shorts all day, but my workplace was a gymnasium! The high school guys gladly included me in their scrimmages and shooting contests. My knee injury from college had finally healed, but I occasionally wore an elastic wrap on it because it still felt a little weaker than my other knee. I held my own against the high school boys as long as I didn't try to drive inside against their taller, stronger bodies. The biggest adjustment was getting used to the shouts of *"Miss Millbern, I'm open!"* instead of being called "Debbie" during scrimmages.

One day a senior member of the boys' varsity basketball team asked if I would work with him on his free throw shooting. He was struggling with his

technique. Brad Michaels was Hollywood handsome---
tall and well-built, with thick dark hair and bright green
eyes. When he smiled, he reminded me of a model on
the cover of *GQ* magazine with his square chin and
dimples on each side of his mouth.

Brad and I separated ourselves from the rest of the
noon-time players and worked on his free throws at a
side basket. He was an eager student and gracious
young man. We chatted and kidded during our brief
training sessions. Because of his focus and willingness
to learn, he began improving his shooting percentage.
This was his senior season of basketball and he told me
that wanted to be the best that he could be. I could
certainly relate to his goal.

Two weeks after I had begun my sessions with Brad,
I was sitting in my apartment watching television.
"*Gunsmoke*" was on, but I wasn't really paying much
attention to it as I was busy organizing a badminton
tournament for my fourth-period class. My apartment
was small, but comfortable. I had bought furniture at
various rummage sales and consignment shops.
Nothing matched, but I was proud to have outfitted my
entire apartment for under $800. I had a beige sofa,
pecan coffee table, rust-colored side chair and a small
drop-leaf dining table. Two twin beds and a gold-
painted dresser filled my only bedroom. I had made a
small bookcase using concrete blocks and four
unfinished shelving planks. Displayed on it were a few
family pictures, college awards, and half-burnt candles.
A huge framed canvas picture filled the wall above the
sofa. It was a view of a farm field and distant barn with
a broken down wagon in the foreground. Mom and

Dad had given me one of their old televisions. My apartment was not fancy, but it was all mine.

It was a little after 9:00 p.m. when I heard my doorbell ring. I peered through the security hole in my door and saw Brad Michaels. I opened the door. Brad stood in the hallway dressed in Levi jeans and a light blue Polo golf shirt.

"Miss Millbern, I really need to talk to you. I've got a problem." His expression was tentative and he diverted his eyes to his brown Sperry Top-Sider shoes.

I motioned Brad to the sofa. A whiff of English Leather aftershave filled the entry hallway as he passed by me. I turned off the television and sat down beside him.

"What's wrong, Brad?" I inquired.

He proceeded to tell me about his mother who had been diagnosed with breast cancer. He shared his feelings about the pain and suffering she was enduring, and how her depression was affecting the family. I sat in silence as he poured his heart out to me. His persona as a big, strapping athlete was fading to a boy-like state of emotion and vulnerability. I contributed words of encouragement that seemed trite and ineffective. Thankfully no one in my family had suffered from any life-threatening diseases, so I was searching for the right words to counsel him. I felt my statements might be precarious to Brad's delicate emotional state. I had no script for this, unlike when I was coaching him and found it easy to let instructional dialogue slip off my tongue. Statements like "keep your elbow under the ball" and "concentrate on the front of the rim" were more my more natural repertoire.

We sat in silence for a few minutes as I searched for more appropriate, consoling remarks. Brad sat leaning forward with his elbows resting on his knees. He seemed nervous as he kept clenching and unclenching his fists. Suddenly he leaned over and gently placed his lips on mine. My initial shock was subdued as I found myself kissing him back. I felt his hand slide under my blouse and cup my breast in his palm. I felt a sexual charge as I got lost in the thrill. He gently pushed me back onto the sofa. With a sudden jerk I sat upright as sensibility overtook my passion. He sat up with a start and an expression of surprise.

"What's wrong?" he asked. He gazed at me with an intense ardor that was temporarily mesmerizing.

"Brad, this is wrong," I responded as I pulled down and smoothed my blouse.

"Don't you find me attractive, Debbie?" It startled me to hear him call me by my first name.

I had to be honest. "Yes, I do. But this can't happen."

"Why?" he asked. His green eyes displayed an inviting softness.

"Because I'm a teacher, and you're a student."

"But I'm eighteen and you're only twenty-two. You're only four years older than me, and I'm very attracted to you."

"Brad, I can't help that. We cannot date."

He stood and had that same overwrought look that I remembered seeing in the face of Greg Stokes when I turned down his marriage proposal in college.

Brad continued speaking. "Wait a minute. What if we were away from Northside High School. Would that make a difference?"

I hesitated for a moment. "Perhaps it would. But we're *not* away from Northside." I stood and pointed to the door. "You have to go and never come to my apartment again. And, our training sessions are over." I marched toward the door and pulled it open. "You're a great guy, Brad, but this just won't work."

Brad walked slowly to the door and left without saying another word. I closed the door and could hear his footsteps disappear down the hall. I flopped back onto the sofa and covered my eyes with my hands. I wasn't sure what to feel. Brad was fun, sensitive, and remarkably mature. I was attracted to him. He was correct in debating our age difference as being irrelevant for a relationship. When I would be thirty-four, he'd be thirty. At forty-four, he'd be forty. It was the situation of teacher/student that would result in dire consequences. Here was a relationship that I would have enjoyed pursuing, but the circumstances were wrong. The timing had been misaligned with Greg; now Brad. My luck with men had not gone well so far.

*****

An extraordinary event occurred in September, 1973. Bobby Riggs, a fifty-five-year-old retired professional tennis player, seized an opportunity to make money and elevate the popularity of tennis. Playing the male chauvinist, he challenged Billie Jean King, a top-ranked female player to a nationally-televised tennis match. She was twenty-nine years old. Riggs claimed that the female game was inferior to the men's game, and that a top female player could not beat a fifty-five-year-old male "washed up" professional player. His taunts prompted King to take him on, especially since she was anxious to promote the status of women tennis players. The purse was billed as $100,000 "winner take all," which was more money than King had earned in thirty-one tournaments. No woman in history had been show-cased in such a spectacle as Riggs hit the talk show circuit and confidently launched his sexist tirade. Called the "Battle of the Sexes," everyone was talking about the match and had an opinion. Men competing against women on a public stage was a new phenomenon.

I watched the build-up to the match with extreme fascination. Riggs's outrageous, almost villainous comments about women athletes angered me. I was outraged at his sexist pronouncements. Having competed against men my entire life, this heavily-publicized event re-ignited a competitive fervor in me. I wanted Billie Jean to not only beat him, but embarrass him.

The match was part comedy show, athletic competition, and sociological phenomenon. King was transported into the Houston Astrodome in front of the 30,000 spectators in a Cleopatra-style chair, carried aloft by four bare-chested muscle men dressed like ancient slaves. Riggs followed in a rickshaw pulled by a bevy of scantily-clad models. Along with 90 million other television viewers, I was glued to the television. I was horrified at the overdramatized spectacle, yet encouraged that there was such massive interest in watching a woman compete.

Billie Jean's strategy of staying at the baseline and running Riggs all over the court was masterful. She won, 6-4, 6-3, 6-3. I wasn't sure what was accomplished by this spectacle other than providing a cathartic release from the real-life conflicts that were afflicting the nation. The country was weary from the Vietnam War, race riots, Watergate, and rising unemployment. Still, the match created controversy. Men sports journalists downplayed King's victory and wrote that Billie Jean should challenge a man her own age as a true measure of women's sports abilities (even though Billie Jean hadn't initiated the challenge against Riggs). Women applauded her victory as an advancement for the status of women athletes. King later stated: "I thought it would set us back fifty years if I didn't win that match. It would ruin the women's tennis tour and affect all women's self-esteem."

Was Billie Jean's win a victory for women, for tennis, or for general youthfulness? I felt strongly that women deserved equal opportunities to compete, but should be able to do so against other *women,* rather than their abilities being compared to men.

*****

Not having much experience with the sport of volleyball, I prepared for my first coaching endeavor in that sport by reading books over the summer on techniques and strategies of volleyball. As a physical education major in college, I had taken a class to learn the basics of the game, but I felt that there was much more to learn in order to be a respectable coach. There were many more variables for me to master since I hadn't competed in the sport. However, core athletic talent, mental toughness, and focus carry over to many sports. Those traits I understood well.

The first task was to conduct tryouts for the team. I had fifty girls show up to try out for the ten spots on the varsity team. Since I knew none of them by name, I had them put masking tape on the backs of their shirts and print their last names on the tape with a black marker. As I ran them through setting, spiking, jumping, and passing drills, it was easy to identify the girls who were not athletic. That made the first cut easy. The final cut was more difficult. But, as I got to know the girls' personalities, attitude and aggressiveness emerged as important components. I had been around enough sports to be able to identify athleticism and innate competitiveness.

The morning that I posted the final ten names on the bulletin board outside my office I could hear a flurry of activity as the girls came to check the list. Shrieks of excitement and disappointment were intermingled with muffled conversations. I heard one girl exclaim in a very loud voice---"I can't believe she cut Shondell!" Another voice chimed in---"What? Boy, *that* took a lot of guts."

In a moment of panic I pulled out my tryout notes and looked for my comments written next to the Shondell name. Reading through them I felt relieved. Kim Shondell was a legitimate cut according to my notes. Her skills were not very good.

That afternoon in the teachers' lounge I asked a few teachers why it would be questionable to cut Kim Shondell from the volleyball team since her name meant nothing to me. They told me that the Shondell name was legendary in the national collegiate volleyball scene. Dr. Don Shondell was the head men's volleyball coach at Ball State University, which was a contender for the NCAA championship each year. He wrote books on volleyball and was considered the dean of volleyball coaches. His sons were terrific athletes--- one currently played on the Ball State men's volleyball team, and the younger one was a basketball player at Northside. Kim Shondell was his only daughter.

In the next few days, neither Dr. Shondell nor Kim came to see me to question my decision to cut her from the team. Whereas I looked like a saint for refraining from letting outside influences sway my selection of the team, I actually acted out of pure ignorance. I selected the ten *best* athletes. In completing my first tryout session as a coach, I couldn't help but reflect on my own tryout for the USA Basketball Team a few years earlier, when politics had definitely influenced the selection of players.

*****

My first year of teaching and coaching flew by. It was an exhausting yet satisfying year in which I learned a lot and felt that I had developed a good teaching and coaching style. I loved going to work everyday and facing the challenges of working with high school students. Because of Title IX, the Indiana High School Athletic Association (IHSAA) had instituted state championships in a variety of girls' sports. My volleyball team made it to the state quarterfinals, losing to Mishawaka Marian High School, which went on to win the state championship. This experience whetted our appetites to improve and go even farther next year. My basketball team was very young and inexperienced, but learned what skills they needed to develop to become better players. I loved coaching them. Fortunately most of my tennis girls belonged to tennis clubs that provided private lessons, so my primary task as their coach was to fill out the match line-up card and stay out of their way.

Switching from coaching volleyball to basketball to tennis without a break between seasons had been challenging. It involved shifting from the emotional and physical let-down of ending a season with one group of athletes to the challenge of motivating a new group. Most of the time I had one weekend between seasons. And the cheerleaders? Their "season" lasted the entire school year. They had a banner year. No one flipped onto her head or got pregnant.

Just like when I was a competitive athlete and now as a coach, I couldn't wait for the next school year.

Working in my gym office at Muncie Northside High School

CHAPTER 12

STATE CHAMPS

"Wow, get a look at him!" Janie Wierks leaned over and whispered into my ear.

Janie and I were sitting together at one of the cafeteria tables during the first-day faculty meeting, listening to Mr. Lemna go over information for the new school year. The delicious aroma of cinnamon rolls filled the air as the lunch staff had come in early to prepare coffee and rolls for the meeting. The floor and tables were shiny, the one time of the year that a residue of stickiness would not coat the floor and tables. Mr. Lemna had just asked the new faculty members to stand so that they could be introduced when Janie whispered to me.

Janie Wierks was my co-teacher in girls' physical education. She was short and petite with strawberry blonde hair and a pleasant smile. She had several pock marks on her face, most likely a result of teenage acne. Janie coached swimming, gymnastics, track, and sponsored the dance team, the sports that I had turned down during my interview. She and I worked well together, and, like me, she was single. We shared an office and had together survived our first full year of teaching. We felt like veterans as we worked in the locker room and equipment closet earlier that morning, organizing for the new school year. We changed the locks on all of the lockers and counted balls, bats, rackets, stopwatches, nets, and orange cones---all the tools of our trade. Everything in the locker room and our office was organized and spotless as we made our way to the cafeteria for the faculty meeting. Like the cafeteria, this would be the neatest and cleanest our working space would be all year.

I didn't look up from writing on my pad of paper when Janie whispered to me. I was engrossed in planning my first volleyball practice of the season, and was half-listening to Mr. Lemna's monotonous instructions about attendance sheets, curriculum changes, and lunch duty assignments. "*Make sure you get your equipment requisitions turned in by October 1. The lost and found is now located in the Dean's office. Soda pop is no longer allowed beyond the east hallway.*"

"Why is he reading everything to us that's already in the faculty handbook?" I mumbled to Janie. "Doesn't he think we can read?" I continued diagramming spiking and passing drills in my notebook.

"Debbie, *look* at the new special education teacher. He is *so* cute!" Janie exclaimed as she whispered more intently to me and added a jab into my ribs with her elbow.

As much as I liked Janie, she was much more man-crazy than I was. She often shared information about her dating escapades. I wondered how she even found the time to date *anyone* last year. Her responsibilities were comparable to mine with her teaching load and coaching, yet I found it hard to squeeze in time to do my grocery shopping, let alone go on a date. I hadn't gone out with anyone in over a year. After the school year ended last June I spent the summer taking a full load of graduate classes, working toward my master's degree in physical education at Ball State University. Luckily the campus was less than a mile from my apartment. I rode my bicycle to class everyday in the sweltering heat, and spent many evenings at the campus library.

One of the classes I took was "Advanced Coaching Strategies in Volleyball." It was taught by Dr. Don Shondell. On the first day of class when Dr. Shondell was reading aloud the names on the class roll, he stopped abruptly after reading my name. I squirmed in my seat, nervously anticipating what he was going to say next. He peered over his glasses at me as I warily raised my hand to acknowledge my presence.

"Ah, Debbie Millbern," he said. "The young coach who had the guts to cut my daughter from the high school volleyball team." The rest of the class shifted their attention to me. The guy sitting next to me whispered, "You did *what*?"

I nodded my head to Dr. Shondell and delivered a weak smile.

"Don't worry, Miss Millbern. Kim was never very good at volleyball, so you can relax." A tidal wave of relief engulfed me.

Dr. Shondell and I became good friends and I attribute much of my volleyball knowledge to him. To my surprise he had attended the previous year's state volleyball finals and watched my team lose its quarterfinal match. During the summer class he gave me suggestions as to adjustments that I could have made that might have impacted the outcome. I appreciated his candor. "Experience is always a good teacher," he told me.

Near the end of summer and just before the start of my second year of teaching, I took a must-needed break and flew to Florida to visit my parents. They had moved to North Miami Beach during the previous year. Dad had purchased a mattress franchise, and Mom worked in the office as his bookkeeper. By now my older brother Mike had graduated from medical school, Tim was in college, and only my littlest brother, David, was still at home finishing high school in Miami. Once David graduated, none of us siblings had graduated from the same high school---four kids; four towns; four high schools. In my twelve years of primary and secondary school, I calculated that I had attended eight different schools. As a result of my frequent moves, I now found myself as a teacher going overboard to make "new" students feel comfortable at Northside.

It was fun spending time with Mom and Dad. I felt so grown up sharing my experiences in teaching and coaching with them. I was finally an *adult* talking to other *adults*, who just happened to be my parents. It seemed weird. They listened intently to my stories and marveled that I had taken my volleyball team to the state finals my first year on the job. They could tell how happy I was. They seemed equally happy to be away from the brutal winters of the Midwest and enjoyed the warm Florida climate.

By the time I finally looked up at Janie's urging to see the new faculty members, they were all seated and blocked from my view by the mass of faculty and staff. I had missed out on seeing this new special education teacher who had caused Janie's excited squeals. When the faculty meeting was over, I hurried to the gymnasium to unpack the box of volleyball team uniforms. Meeting this hot new teacher would have to wait.

*****

Since all of the players on last year's volleyball team were underclassmen, I had everyone coming back for our second season together. I held a brief tryout for new players, most of which were freshmen. Since I also formed a junior varsity team to develop young players, I could move players up and down as they improved or regressed. I could tell from the onset that this team was focused. They were a competitive group of girls who immediately established a goal to win the state championship this year. They had gotten a taste of success last season and were willing to work hard. I knew this was an attainable goal as long as everyone stayed healthy. "Anything is possible," I told them. "If you work hard and stay focused, we can get there together."

In the three sports I coached at Northside, there was a level of comfort between the athletes and me. I had very high expectations but was not excessively demanding. I didn't yell at them a lot. All it took from me was a *look* for a player to know if she had screwed up. They knew that I had been a competitive athlete who understood what it took to succeed. There was mutual respect between us. Coaching involves a delicate balance of strictness and compassion. In my development and evolution as a coach, I was learning when to push and when to hold back. It is a fine line that takes experience. During games I outwardly demonstrated confidence and calmness to the players, even though my insides were swirling like a tornado. I found that a wink, a smile, and a "thumbs-up" to a panicky athlete worked wonders. I truly loved these kids and wanted them to understand and experience the joys, commitment, and perseverance it takes to be a winning athlete. Along with competing, I insisted on good sportsmanship and respect between my players and our opponents. At the end of last season we had received a letter from the Mishawaka Marian volleyball team that defeated us in the state quarterfinals.

"Muncie Northside, you were not only the best competition we faced all year, but you exhibited the most outstanding sportsmanship before, throughout, and at the conclusion of the match," they wrote.

I was proud to read this letter to my team. "Dignity and humility in winning *and* losing," I said as I held the letter up in front of them.

Another area in which I felt strongly was the appearance of the girls when we traveled to "away" games. I wanted them to be proud to be aggressive *female* athletes, without the need to dress, look, or act like men. My past experiences observing the male-like appearances of some of my female athlete friends had affected me. During one of our early meetings I told the players that they were to dress nicely when we traveled to contests. I didn't feel a need to enforce as strict a dress code as my physical education professors had required of me, but I didn't want a group of ragamuffins walking into an opponent's gymnasium. Hypocritical? Maybe a little, but with the explosion of girls' sports, we were on a new stage of visibility, and I wanted the girls to be equally proud of their femininity *and* competitiveness. They were the new role models for little girls who aspired to be athletes.

"A skirt would be appropriate," I said. "You may play like beasts on the court, but I want you to look like ladies off the court." After my pronouncement I noticed some nervous glances between a few of the players.

Jeri, one of the players who I suspected to be a lesbian, slowly raised her hand. "Coach, would nice slacks be okay?" Her question was followed by muffled giggles from the rest of the team.

I stifled an urge to laugh. "Jeri, dress slacks with a nice top will be fine. But absolutely no tattered jeans or sloppy, over-sized T-shirts!"

Jeri responded with a sigh of relief and gave a discreet hand slap to Paula, who was sitting next to her.

To be brutally honest, the team consisted of feminine-looking girls. They were good students, and many had boyfriends. When they hit the court, however, I loved that they were relentless, hard-core athletes. This thrilled me because I had tried to model this same behavior. Gender-role conflicts were a reality in this new world of girls' sports. I had experienced these conflicts myself. Can one retain her femininity and be a good athlete? Are boys turned off by female athleticism? Is it okay to beat a boy in a sport? It was a dilemma that continued to linger. During casual conversations and interactions with my team, these questions sometimes came up, albeit subtly. I knew they looked to me for support and guidance.

*****

The newness of coaching kept me focused on continually learning how and improving on ways to motivate teenage girls to compete, as well as learning the strategies of each sport that I was assigned to coach. Basketball was second-nature to me, but volleyball and tennis took a lot of study. When coming up for air from the daily tasks of coaching, I sometimes experienced frustrations at the inequalities that still existed between boys' and girls' sports. Even though the Title IX law establishing equal opportunities had been in effect for over two years, we were still treated like second-class citizens. As a first-year coach, I hadn't complained. I was grateful for anything and everything. We had bus transportation to away games, licensed referees, money for a fast-food meal on the way home, and uniforms. The athletic director scheduled the contests, set up the scoring and timing equipment, and paid the officials. I thought it was unfair, however, that the gymnasium was reserved for boys' team practices ahead of the girls. Many times we were forced to practice before school at 5:30 or 6:00 a.m., while the boys' teams got the best time slots---after school and early evening. We also had to use the same uniforms for volleyball, basketball, and track. We simply passed them on to the next team at the end of each season. We had no warm-up jackets or pants. Also, Janie Wierks and I each coached three sports, whereas the men teachers at our school who were head coaches were assigned to only one sport, or at the most, were an assistant coach for a second sport. We didn't have assistant coaches. In fact, I coached both the varsity *and* junior varsity teams in all three of my sports. I didn't want to cause a ruckus or be identified as a whiner, but my enthusiasm waned at times due to pure exhaustion and frustration. I tried to be diplomatic when asking the athletic director for equipment or money for extra things. If we wanted extras he told me that we would have to earn it on our own. So, we held bake sales and car washes. I never saw a boys' team have to do either.

One sunny Saturday in the fall, my volleyball team held a car wash to earn enough money to travel to a distant tournament in which I felt we needed to compete. We had two girls on the street waving huge signs beckoning motorists. The remaining team members were relegated to washing and drying cars in a gas station parking lot. I noticed that we weren't getting much business. So, I pulled an admittedly sexist strategy from my repertoire and asked Kasey and Annie, the two cutest girls on the team (who *happened* to be wearing very brief shorts and tank tops), to replace Jeri and Paula, who were waving the signs on the street (who *happened* to be wearing baggy, cut-off jeans and oversized T-shirts). It was a brilliant substitution as business picked up immediately. Even though I despised sexism, I swallowed my pride to use it temporarily for the benefit of the team travel budget.

*****

One Sunday evening in October I received a phone call from a woman named Maxine Thayer. She told me that there was an AAU women's basketball team in Indianapolis and they wanted me to play on their team. Maxine was the manager of the team, handling the scheduling, uniforms, and other organizational tasks. A man named Stu was the coach. The team practiced on Sunday afternoons throughout the fall, and then played games against other AAU teams around the Midwest during the winter---also on Sundays. She told me there was an AAU National Tournament every spring. I remembered back when I met Harley Redin, the coach of the Wayland Hutcherson Flying Queens. He had touted the superiority of the women players on the AAU circuit.

I was excited at the prospect of playing again. The drive to the Indianapolis recreation center where we practiced and played took a little over an hour. I knew it would be a major commitment, but I wasn't ready to totally give up basketball. The game still was in my blood. I proceeded to devote my Sunday afternoons and evenings to play for the Marion-Kay Peppers. The sponsor, who owned a spice distribution factory, paid our travel expenses and I soon bonded with a great group of women who loved the game as much as I did. All of the women had jobs. They were office and factory workers, teachers, recreation center directors, and bank tellers. A few of the gals on the team had played against me during college, so we enjoyed reminiscing about past games.

Competing had its drawbacks, however. Sunday had been my only day of rest and recovery from the toils of teaching and coaching all week. So, my day of rest was gone. However, I found the experience to be invigorating, both mentally and physically, as I re-discovered my joy of playing basketball. Like re-uniting with a lover, it was pure rapture, and I found myself surprisingly refreshed to start the new week on Monday mornings. Playing basketball on a team once again was actually a shot in the arm that revitalized me.

*****

After a month of school I finally had the opportunity to meet that special education teacher with whom Janie Wierks was so enamored. He was sitting in the cafeteria eating lunch with a few other male teachers. I rarely ate lunch in the cafeteria, preferring to bring my own sandwich from home and eat in my office while grading papers or preparing afternoon lesson plans. That day I had forgotten my lunch and went into the cafeteria to grab something. I chose a salad with lettuce, chicken, cucumbers, and carrots. The plastic bowl was shrink-wrapped so solidly with cellophane that I thought it might take a blow-torch to open it. The cafeteria noise was at a high decibel level with the combined sounds of clanging dishes and vivacious teenagers. The deafening sound reminded me why I preferred eating in the solitude of my office. I sat down at the teachers' table next to Dallas Kunkle, who taught social studies. Dallas and I had become good friends because he would call and ask me to play basketball with some of the male teachers on occasional Saturday afternoons when none of us had coaching commitments. Dallas was the assistant boys' cross country and baseball coach.

"Have you met Jim Powers? Dallas asked me, pointing to a dark-haired man sitting across the table.

"No, I haven't had the pleasure," I said as I reached across and shook Jim's hand. "Nice to meet you and welcome to Northside."

Janie was right. Jim Powers was handsome. He had thick, wavy hair that was just long enough that it barely touched the tops of his ears. He was small in stature, but fit-looking with brown eyes and an infectious smile. Whereas many of the male teachers wore open-collared sport shirts to work, Jim was wearing a white dress shirt with a striped tie. Not only was he nice looking, but his professionalism was impressive.

He half-stood as he shook my hand. "You're the girls' PE teacher, aren't you?"

Wow, I thought with an inkling of sarcasm. *He's smart, too.....since I'm wearing shorts and tennis shoes!*

"Yes. Janie Wierks and I teach PE. We're both in our second year here." As I spoke, I tugged on the cellophane to uncover my salad and watched lettuce and cucumbers fly onto the table and floor.

The expression on Jim's face was light-hearted. "That's why eating salad keeps you thin. You only get to eat about half of it."

I chuckled as I struggled to open the tiny salad dressing packet. I was praying that I wouldn't spray blue cheese dressing over everyone.

"So you teach special ed?" I asked as I slowly dribbled the thin white dressing over what was left of my salad.

"Yep. They assigned me to a room directly across from the office so they can keep an eye on my kids." He winked at me as he spoke.

"Maybe they want to keep an eye on *you*," Dallas chimed in with a hearty guffaw.

We all laughed as the bell ending the lunch period blasted into the cafeteria, interrupting all conversations. Students grabbed their books and scurried out the door. I grabbed what was left of my salad and bid farewell to Jim and the other teachers. They scattered to their respective classrooms as well, and the cafeteria became quiet. All that was left were tables and a floor that resembled a trash dump where wild animals had scavenged.

*****

As the volleyball season progressed, I could tell that this year's team was special. The team chemistry was good and their passing, setting, and spiking skills were improving with every match. They played with extreme confidence, but without the swagger of discourtesy toward opponents. I worked the girls hard in practice and they often begged for more drills. By mid-season we were undefeated. We were getting small write-ups in the *Muncie Star* newspaper. The crowds were growing larger at our games, and it wasn't solely parents sitting in the stands. Teachers, students, and community members began attending our matches. I even saw Jim Powers and Dallas Kunkle at a few matches. When I told Janie that I had finally met the new special education teacher, she started blabbering … "I heard he has dated some of the student teachers." …

"I sure would like to go out with him." ... "Do you suppose he is serious about anyone?"

"Janie, catch your breath!" I interrupted her as I shook my head and laughed. "Jeez, get control of yourself!" Janie was obsessed with Jim Powers, and I was obsessed with winning a state championship.

An interesting phenomenon occurred as we played our final season matches. A small group of Northside male students began sitting together at our home matches and cheering for the girls. Like an organized cheerblock they chanted and stomped their feet in various rhythms. I had never seen this---a boys' cheerblock supporting a *girls'* team! They were primarily the male athletes and popular boys at the school which made it even more impressive. The girls were thrilled to have generated this level of interest from their male counterparts. Whereas many teenage girls might feel self-conscious performing in front of a group of teenage boys, my team did not. They thrived on it and played even better. More important, I was sensing a gradual cultural shift in the way female athletes were being perceived in society. Along with this, my opinion on cheerleading was softening since *boys* were now leading cheers for the *girls*!

We were 14-0 heading into the sectionals. To make it to the eight-team state finals we would have to win both the sectional and regional tournaments. Having made it to the state finals the previous year helped the girls understand the importance of being ready for every match and maintaining their poise for the next three weekends. I realized that anytime a team is undefeated, the pressure continues to elevate with each match. To my surprise we breezed through both the sectional and regional and were state tournament-bound for the second year in a row. The boys' cheerblock continued to expand at every match.

The Monday after we won the regional, our athletic director, Mr. Carmichael, came to my office and handed me a small cardboard box stuffed with new blue- and red-striped hand towels. Mr. Carmichael had the difficult job of balancing practice facilities and monies among all of the boys' and girls' sports teams. He had the insurmountable task of trying to keep all of the coaches happy. So far, I had found him to be respectful of me, most likely because I didn't complain or whine. I was not overly demanding.

"Give these bench towels to the girls. They've earned 'em," he said. "No team from this school has been to two state championships. Congratulations!"

I stared at the towels. It was a thoughtful token for our accomplishments, but I secretly wished the box would have been filled with warm-up jackets that I had been requesting for over a year.

When I distributed the towels to the girls at practice, you would have thought that I handed them gold watches. They jumped and screamed, hugging the towels to their chests. It made me realize how appreciative girl athletes are to anything given to them. Their innocent gratitude was refreshing compared to many of the male athletes who often displayed attitudes of entitlement.

At the state finals there would be eight regional winners, making it necessary to win three matches in one day to be crowned state champions. It would be a full day of volleyball starting with morning quarterfinals and ending with the final match that evening. The previous year we had lost our first match in the morning but stayed all day to watch the finals. This year we vowed that it would be different. Our goal was to win it all. Parents, teachers, students, and our boys' cheerblock followed our team bus in a caravan to Indianapolis. The date was November 23, 1974.

Much to my surprise, we won our first two matches quite easily. A volleyball match is the best-of-three games, and we beat both Fort Wayne Wayne and West Lafayette Harrison each in two games. The finals were to be against South Bend Riley at 8:30 p.m. Riley came into the final match with an 18-1 record.

The state championship match was very exciting. Riley won the first game. It was obvious to me that my girls were tight and playing tentatively. Before the start of the second game I gave them a pep talk. Amid the thunderous chants of our boys' cheerblock and the screaming Riley fans, I gathered the team in a tight huddle and knelt down in the middle of them.

"We've come too far to let this slip away!" I shouted as I looked into the eyes of each player. "We're only two games short of our goal! Get out there and beat on them! Play *your* game! I *know* you can do it!" I saw their expressions of panic melt away as they nodded their heads and broke from the huddle.

We came to life in the second game, jumped out to a quick lead, and finished them off. The momentum had shifted to us, but the third and deciding game was a fierce battle. I struggled to maintain my composure as we lost the first few points. With the girls glancing at me for my reaction, I stood, smiled at them, and pumped my fist enthusiastically into the air.

"Here we go, Northside! Now we go!" I shouted to them. My stomach was in knots. The Northside fans were on their feet screaming and chanting. It was deafening, so I knew that my body language and facial expressions would convey more to my team than yelling, because *everyone* in the arena was yelling at them. I wanted them to look at me and see that I had confidence in them. With powerful serving and outstanding defense, we finally began pulling ahead. I continued to stand and clap for their good plays and give an encouraging "that's okay" head nod when they lost a point. Their confidence was building as their spikes became more fierce and their blocks higher over the net. I stood in awe of these girls' competitive savvy since they had so little athletic experience. None of them had played competitive sports before high school. The bench players and I held hands tightly as our only freshman on the team served an ace to Riley's court for the winning point.

With reckless abandon I ran onto the floor and began hugging the girls. The blue- and red-striped towels were tossed into the air. We all jumped up and down, hugging and crying. Before I realized what was happening, the girls lifted me onto their shoulders. Members of the boys' cheerblock stormed onto the court. Not only were we state champions with a perfect 22-0 record, but we were bringing Muncie Northside High School its very first *girls'* Indiana state championship trophy.

Playing in the 1974 State Championship

Northside Titans win!

1974 Indiana Girls' Volleyball State Champions

CHAPTER 13

JIM POWERS

I heard the telephone ringing inside my apartment as I frantically searched for my key buried somewhere in my gym bag. I was still wearing my Marion-Kay Pepper basketball uniform. The church hall where we played our game in Chicago that afternoon did not have a showering facility, so I had driven the four hours home with three things on my mind----a hot shower, food, and a warm bed. It was almost 6:00 p.m. and already dark outside. The winter months brought early nightfall to Indiana. After struggling to open the door, I rushed to answer the phone, leaving the door ajar.

"Hello?" I asked. My voice was abrupt and short as I caught my breath from my dashing across the living room.

"Is this Debbie?" I heard the male voice ask.

"Yes it is," I answered.

"This is Jim Powers, and I was wondering if you were going to Charlie Marcus's mother's calling hours."

I hesitated as I processed the information. Jim Powers *(the special education teacher)*....Charlie Marcus *(our assistant principal)*. Mr. Marcus's mother had died last week and her calling hours were tonight at the funeral home. I knew about her death, but hadn't planned on going since I knew that I would be playing a basketball game in Chicago, and was doubtful that I would make it back in time. In fact, the event had escaped my mind.

"I really don't know," I answered. "I just now got back into town."

"Well, if you want to go, I would be happy to swing by and pick you up," Jim said.

I stood silent for a moment and ran my fingers through my hair. My clothes were sweat-stained. My hair was dirty, and I was tired. But a pang of guilt of *not* attending the calling hours entered my brain, along with a visual image of Jim Powers.

"Sure. Let me get a quick shower. Would a half-hour be okay?"

"No problem. I'll be there in thirty minutes," he responded.

Being an athlete and physical education major, I was an expert at quick showering. Sometimes I had only fifteen minutes between classes at Indiana University to shower and walk across campus to my next class. As I was blow-drying my hair, I thought about Janie Wierks. *She'll just die,* I chuckled to myself, *when she finds out that Jim Powers called me.*

I pulled a navy wool skirt from the closet and paired it with a white silk blouse and light blue button down cardigan sweater. With a quick whisk of mascara and lipstick, I was good to go. Somehow the fatigue I felt twenty minutes ago had evaporated.

Jim pulled up in front of my apartment in an orange Volkswagen Beetle. A light snow was falling, but not enough to stick to the ground. In January it seemed like snow was an everyday occurrence, sometimes in the form of a blizzard and other times a light frosting.

"Funny," I said to Jim as I climbed into the passenger seat. "I have a *red* Volkswagen Beetle."

"I know," Jim said. "I've seen you driving around in it."

There was a large crowd at the funeral home, a gathering made up of many teachers and staff from Northside High School, as well as extended family of Mr. Marcus. Jim and I chatted with several teachers as we stood in line waiting our turn to convey our condolences to the Marcus family. I looked around for Janie Wierks but didn't see her. I wondered if the other teachers noticed that Jim and I had come together.

So what? I thought. *They probably assume we arrived at the funeral home at the same time. And why should anyone really care about Jim and me being together? And besides, Janie Wierks would be the only one who would take special notice.*

When we were ready to leave, Jim asked if I was hungry. I was actually starving, since it had been a full basketball game and a long drive home from Chicago since I had eaten.

"Not only am I hungry, but I'm famished!" I told him.

"Good. So am I. Let's head to Pizza King."

If anyone wants good pizza in Muncie, Indiana, they go to the Pizza King. With plastic checkerboard tablecloths, wooden chairs, and brick interior walls, it is a homey local establishment. Brightly colored Tiffany light fixtures dangle above each table. It is where parents with little kids go for a special family night out and where teenagers gather after Friday night football games. The aroma of sausage and onions permeate the air a block away. Inside, you place your order by dialing a bright red telephone attached to your table.

"A large royal-feast pizza and a pitcher of beer," Jim spoke into the phone receiver as he looked directly at me. His widened eyes and nodding head indicated that he was searching for my approval.

"Perfect. My favorite!" I reassured him after he hung up.

The next several hours were filled with conversation about our experiences at Northside High School. Since it was his first year, and my second at the school, we had a lot to share about our transitions from being college students to teachers. We talked a little about our families. He told me about his two older brothers, one of which had Down syndrome and still lived at home with his parents. He had no sisters. It was easy to talk to Jim. He was interested in my background as an athlete and was surprised that I found time to continue playing on a basketball team. Even though he was not involved in coaching at Northside, he talked about being the top track and cross country athlete in his high school and how he was an avid baseball fan. Since he liked sports, a portion of our conversation revolved around my volleyball team's recent state championship.

"That trophy has to be four foot tall!" he exclaimed.

He was right. The state championship trophy was so large that Mr. Lemna removed two shelves in the trophy case to make it fit. Since the school was only a few years old, there were only a few trophies and plaques in the huge wooden case. The boys' wrestling team had won the school's only other state championship the previous year.

"Yeah, it looks kinda lonely in that trophy case," I responded. "But with all the great athletes at Northside, I'm sure many more trophies will be added. In fact, I hope to add another four-footer next year."

Glancing at our watches, we were both shocked to see how late it had become. Couples had come and gone at the tables around us, but we had been oblivious to them. A silver pizza pan with a few scattered crumbs and two empty beer pitchers and mugs were the only items remaining on our table when we left at 11:30.

When we arrived in front of my apartment Jim kept the car running. One fact about Volkswagens is that the heater and the defroster kick in only after driving for about ten minutes. So, when first starting out, you have to continually wipe the inside of the windshield to be able to see while driving. I kept an old rag in my car for just that purpose. I noticed that Jim did the same, and we shared the duty of frantically wiping the windshield while Jim peered through the slowly expanding gap on the frosted windshield. Just as we reached my apartment, the car was toasty warm and the windshield was clear.

"How would you like to have dinner with me next Saturday?" Jim asked.

I ran through next week's calendar in my head. Wrestling meet Tuesday night (*I was volunteering to take tickets*)....girls' home basketball game Thursday night (*I was the coach*)....boys' home basketball game Friday night (*I had to supervise the cheerleaders*)....Marion-Kay Peppers game Sunday afternoon (*I was playing*).

"Saturday would be great," I said. "But we just had dinner together *tonight*," I added with a slight tone of sarcasm.

He looked at me with an expression of faint amusement. "That doesn't count. That was a post-funeral snack. Let's talk at school this week to set a time for Saturday." He hesitated. "Hey, thanks for going with me tonight. It was fun."

"Yeah, who ever knew a funeral could be so enjoyable?" I said with a smile.

As I stepped out into the cold air, he leaned over and gave me a quick wave. "See you at school."

I pulled my coat a little tighter as I scurried into the warm apartment building. *Maybe my luck with men is finally changing,* I said to myself.

*****

I was in the middle of our high school basketball season. Coaching both the junior varsity and varsity girls' basketball teams was challenging and tiring since we were assigned either the 8:00 p.m. or the 6:00 a.m. practice slot throughout the winter. The boys' teams got first dibs on the gym. And, home wrestling meets took away several evenings of practice. Not only was the scheduling erratic, but my girls were not very skilled at basketball. Several of the players were carry-overs from the volleyball team. Often when I turned my back on them in practice, they would be setting the basketball back and forth between them as if it was volleyball. They were great kids and athletes, just not into basketball like I was. Plus, they were still basking in the glory of being volleyball state champions. Still, they were improving with each game and we were having a decent season. But there was no way we would make it to the girls' basketball state finals. There were too many teams who were much better. In fact, I doubted that we could win our sectional. Nevertheless, I loved coaching them.

Even though my days at school were busy with classes, cheerleaders, and basketball practice, I found myself thinking about Jim throughout the week. He was bright, handsome, and had a good sense of humor. He was serious about his teaching, but seemed to have a playful side to him. I looked forward to our dinner date on Saturday and the opportunity to get to know him better. I did not tell Janie about my date because I knew it would upset her. Better left unsaid, I figured.

On Saturday morning Dallas Kunkle called and asked if I wanted to play basketball in the afternoon. I loved these pick-up games with the men because it helped me stay in shape for my Marion-Kay Pepper games. We played half court two-on-two with Dallas and I paired up against the boys' track coach and the assistant football coach. After a lively scrimmage I rushed home to get ready for my date. Jim had left a note in my school mailbox that he would pick me up at 6:00. I decided to wear one of my nicest dresses and pair it with black leather boots. I curled my hair and applied makeup---a rarity for me. Jim hadn't indicated where he was taking me for dinner, but I guessed it would be a nice place.

When Jim picked me up he told me that he wanted to show me where he lived. A thin glaze of ice coated the road as we headed out of town on a narrow, dark road. After about fifteen minutes Jim turned into a long gravel driveway. Near the entrance was a dimly lit blue sign: *Camp Isanogel.*

"You live at a camp?" I asked.

"Yep. This is an Easter Seals camp for disabled children. I'm the summer camp director, so they let me live in one of the cabins year-round."

We stopped in front a brown wooden cabin. Adjacent to the cabin and surrounded by a heavy chain-link fence was a large swimming pool covered with a grey tarp. Jim unlatched the green wooden door into his cabin and we walked into a spacious wood-paneled room dimly lit by a bronze floor lamp situated next to a tweed sofa. A wooden rocking chair and heavily scratched coffee table were the only other furniture. On an unfinished plank of wood supported by bricks was a stereo system. A few magazines were strewn around--- *Newsweek, Money, Field & Steam.* In the corner of the room and elevated on a brick hearth was a dark wood-burning stove with a long flue that jutted up through the ceiling planks. Two small windows were adorned with green and brown plaid curtains. Jim walked to the back of the room and opened a door. A Dalmatian bolted through the door and ran across the thick shag carpet to greet me.

"This is Rastus. She's my roommate." Jim scratched Rastus's head as she sniffed at the hem of my dress.

We walked into the small back room where Rastus had been. It had a counter with a hot plate, a sink, and a refrigerator. I opened a cupboard and saw a stack of paper plates, two glasses and a coffee mug. I opened the refrigerator. In it was a bottle of ketchup, one can of beer, and something wrapped in foil. It smelled like fish.

"No wonder you're so skinny," I said as I closed the refrigerator door.

"I'm not much of a cook."

"No kidding," I smirked.

Not seeing a bedroom, I asked, "Where do you sleep?"

He pointed back toward the living room. "The sofa is a hide-a-bed."

"And the bathroom?"

Pointing to a door next to the refrigerator, he said, "Just enough room for a toilet in that closet."

I raised my palms into the air and shrugged my shoulders. "Everything a guy needs!"

Jim grabbed my arm and guided me back toward the front door. "Come on," he said. We walked outside across the grassy side yard toward a large brown building. Rastus tagged along. She stopped to pee, and then ran to catch up with us. The frozen grass was crunchy beneath our shoes. Entering the building I could see that it was the camp dining hall. The tables and benches were neatly stacked against the walls. Two shuffleboard courts were painted on the beige-speckled linoleum. We continued walking through a large swinging door. The kitchen was an enormous stainless steel world of elevated counters, stoves, shelves, and refrigerators. Pots and pan dangled from huge ceiling hooks. Tall wall shelves were stacked with boxes of paper towels, salt and pepper shakers, cooking oil, Jell-O, oatmeal, and macaroni.

"Nice, huh?" Jim said.

"Sure beats your kitchen," I responded.

Jim leaned against the counter and crossed his arms and looked at me. "So what do you want to fix for dinner?"

I stared back at him. There have been only a few times in my life when I have been at a loss for words. This was one of them. *Was he kidding? Did I hear him correctly? Was he asking me to cook dinner?* After collecting my thoughts I responded, "What in the world do you mean?"

"Well....I thought we could run to the grocery and get some food to fix here."

I stared at him in disbelief. "And who is going to fix it?"

An impish grin appeared on his face. "It's obvious that I can't cook."

I was torn between anger and amusement. It angered me that he had the audacity to invite me to dinner and then expect me to cook it in this massive industrial kitchen. Yet I was amused that he would have the nerve to assume that I would do it. It intrigued me that a man would even consider such a bold notion on a first date---especially with a fiercely independent feminist.

My amusement won over my indignation and we proceeded to drive to the store where we bought chicken, vegetables, bread and wine. Thankfully I found an apron in a kitchen drawer to keep the grease from splattering my nice dress as I fried the chicken.

We sat atop stainless steel stools to eat at the massive counter. We talked and drank a lot of wine. Thank goodness for the wine because I wasn't sure I wanted to coherently analyze what I was getting into with this guy.

*****

Two weeks after winning the state championship I made an appointment with Mr. Lemna to discuss my job performance. With strong teaching evaluations and two trips to the state finals I figured that I had enough credibility to be bold. I felt that we women coaches were being overworked and misused, and I planned to tell him so. Title IX was almost three years old and I felt that coaching three sports plus sponsoring the cheerleaders was far beyond the realm of equality when compared to the work load for men coaches. In the meeting with Mr. Lemna I carefully articulated my case and asked to be relieved of coaching girls' tennis and the supervision of cheerleaders. In fairness to him and the school, I told him that I would continue both of those responsibilities through the end of the school year, but desired to coach only volleyball and basketball for the following year. To my mild surprise he agreed without any argument or hesitation. He felt confident that he could find another woman, perhaps even someone outside the school, who might be interested in handling tennis and the cheerleaders. In that same meeting I told him that I was playing on the Marion-Kay Peppers AAU basketball team and that it was likely that we would qualify for the National AAU Championships in the spring. That would necessitate me taking almost a week off school to travel to Gallup, New Mexico, the site of the tournament. Again, he agreed to approve my absence and told me that he was proud of my accomplishments. I was on a roll! I left Mr. Lemna's office feeling happy and relieved. Unlike a few years ago when I complained to the dean at Indiana University about inequities, Title IX was finally making an impact and slowly being implemented. *Interesting that I had to ask, though,* I thought to myself. *Mr. Lemna would probably have changed nothing if I hadn't brought it up. Note to self: ask for things after earning respect.*

*****

Jim and I began spending vast amounts of time together. Many evenings we would watch television at my apartment, have dinner together, work at Northside school events, or listen to music at his cabin. Muncie didn't have a lot of nightlife options for young professionals. The local bar scene favored the nearby college students. At my insistence we occasionally went to a movie. We were spending so much of our free time together that I found myself scrimping on some of my class preparations. Thank goodness I had ready-made lesson plans from the previous year to get me through. In the classroom I continued to be energetic and focused with the students, but I often found myself leaving my school bag inside the front door of my apartment untouched over the entire weekend. I would place it there on Friday evening with good intentions of doing some work, but end up not touching it until I was on my way to school on Monday morning. It was a good thing that I didn't teach English or history, which require an ungodly amount of grading. I had a different attitude; a new yearning was tugging at me. Whereas I used to spend endless hours on class preparations, planning drills, practice stations, lead-up games, and class tournaments, now during my free time I preferred spending time with Jim. My weekends were now devoted to Jim and playing basketball with the Marion-Kay Peppers. I didn't feel guilty, because I was still a committed teacher and coach. Jim's entrance into my life had brought a new dimension, and I was learning balance.

It had become obvious to the Northside teachers and students that Jim and I were dating. When I told Janie Wierks that he and I were seeing each other, she stared at me in disbelief for what seemed like minutes. She finally shrugged her shoulders and told me how lucky I was and that she was happy for me. I was glad that she and I had a strong enough friendship that it didn't affect our work relationship. My students and athletes were all giggly about this new intra-school teacher romance, often asking questions about where we'd gone on our dates and if we were going to get married. They enjoyed teasing and embarrassing me.

On one of our dates Jim revealed that he had wanted to ask me out since the beginning of school. I asked him why he had waited so long. His face transformed into a ridiculous smile. "Are you kidding? I didn't dare bother you until after the volleyball state championship. I could tell how focused you were, so I knew I wouldn't have had a chance."

I wrapped my arms around him. "Smart move, because you were right."

*****

With great anticipation, on January 26, 1975 I tuned into the first nationally-televised women's basketball game. Immaculata College was playing the Maryland Terrapins in College Park, Maryland. I had also encouraged my Northside basketball girls to watch, since this television broadcast was historic. I wanted them to see college women playing basketball on television, something I was never exposed to when I was their age. Jim came to my apartment to watch the game with me. I had explained to him that Immaculata was the team that had defeated my Indiana University team at the 1972 national championships, and they had subsequently won the 1973 and 1974 championships. Tiny Immaculata College was still a powerhouse.

My heart ached with jealousy as I sat glued to the screen watching the players warm up. How I wished that could have been me on that court. During the pre-game interview the male broadcaster asked Maryland's coach, Dottie McKnight, if her players were still interested in boys. I immediately choked on a potato chip, dumbfounded at what I was hearing.

"What the heck?" I yelled at the television. Jim began laughing.

I turned to him. I was seething. "Can you imagine that announcer asking Lefty Driesell, the Maryland *men's* basketball coach, if his players were still interested in *girls*?"

Jim shrugged his shoulders and said nothing while I continued to rant. "Two steps forward with a televised game; one step back with that sexist interview," I mumbled.

During the game I sat mesmerized on the edge of the sofa, taking in the action and the play-by-play commentary. It was a sloppily-played game with a lot of turnovers. Immaculata took a commanding lead. Suddenly with two minutes remaining, the game abruptly disappeared from the screen, interrupted by the opening credits of the movie, *Heidi*.

I screamed at the television as the movie began. "I can't believe this!" Grabbing a pillow off the sofa, I heaved it onto a side chair. "Do you see now what we women have to put up with? This is so wrong!"

Jim looked at me with a kind, sympathetic expression. "Well at least they chose *Heidi*. That's a real nice women's movie," he said softly.

I glared at him trying to decide whether to laugh or smack him. "What a travesty for women's basketball---a lopsided, poorly-played game that is pre-empted by a cheesy movie!" I ranted.

Jim Powers

CHAPTER 14

IS HE THE ONE?

Unlike me, Jim had lived in the same town for most all of his twenty-four years. He was born in Muncie and attended a kindergarten-through-twelfth-grade-school. He went away to college for two years, but moved back to Muncie and finished college at Ball State University, which was one block from his parents' house. And now, of course, he was teaching in Muncie. This was polar opposite from my background, having attended numerous schools in a variety of Indiana towns. My nomadic youth was a foreign concept to him. Whereas Jim's parents resided in the same house where he grew up, my parents' current residence was a penciled number and street in my address book. It seemed like everywhere Jim and I went in Muncie someone knew him, his parents, or his brothers. I met his childhood friends, the parents of his childhood friends, his former teachers, friends and co-workers of his parents, his neighbors, and all of the people one interacts with while growing up in the same town. It was a comforting feeling and gave me reassurance of

Jim's character, since everyone told me what an outstanding guy he was. I also was a little envious that he had so many close friends and long-time acquaintances. It seemed like the fabric of his life consisted of tightly woven threads, whereas mine was a jumble of thin strands. I regretted that I didn't have any lifelong friends. How does one continue a relationship with a best friend in fifth grade or eighth grade when you vanished from their lives after one year?

I finally met Jim's parents one Friday evening when they invited me to their home for dinner. Unlike my parents, who were in their forties, Jim's were older---in their mid-sixties. Their oldest son was married and lived away. Steve, his brother with Down syndrome, lived at home and worked at a local sheltered workshop designated for adults with physical and mental disabilities. Jim's mother was a petite woman and a wonderful cook and housekeeper. She had majored in home economics in college, so the meal was right out of *Good Housekeeping*---pot roast, mashed potatoes and gravy, corn casserole, pear and walnut salad, homemade biscuits, and fresh apple pie.

After Steve was born, Mrs. Powers had gone back to college to get a teaching degree in special education. She worked diligently with Steve every day to improve his speech and language skills, and had recently retired from teaching at a local elementary school. Jim's dad was retired from a local transmission manufacturing plant, where he had worked as the service sales manager for forty-five years. He was a large man with thick, gray hair. Like his wife, he had a soft heart and a gentle soul.

Mr. and Mrs. Powers were very kind and welcoming to me. It was obvious that Jim had grown up in a solid, loving family within the walls of a modest home and amid traditional values. Steve was a sweet, low-functioning guy who smiled and nodded a lot. I had difficulty understanding his speech, so I did a lot of smiling and nodding back to him. Meeting someone's family reveals a lot. Even though Jim's mother had a career outside of the home, it was evident that she maintained the traditions of a devoted housewife and mother. Not only did she dote on her family, but she also was the sole preparer of the meal, had set an elaborate table, cleared the table, and washed the dishes. She jumped up from the table to get more butter, biscuits, or iced tea for anyone in need. The men at the table were definitely being served. This worried me a little because I am more of a "if you want it, get it yourself" kind of girl. Jim, I thought, might have expectations that the feminist side of me would have difficulty fulfilling.

*****

One Sunday afternoon Jim traveled with me to Indianapolis to watch me play a basketball game with my Marion-Kay Peppers team. We were having a good season and I was their leading scorer. That day I scored twenty-one points, and our victory over the Springfield, Illinois team guaranteed us a spot in the upcoming National AAU Tournament. During our drive back to Muncie Jim confessed to me that he was uncomfortable seeing all of the lesbians playing on my team.

"What do you mean...*uncomfortable?*" I asked, unable to disguise the shock in my voice.

"Well, they just look and act like men. It's hard for me to watch that."

I shifted in my seat. "Are you saying that you won't come to watch me play anymore?"

"I like to watch you, but not them."

We rode in silence as I thought about what he had said. I realized that many people are homophobic, but I was certainly not one of them. I viewed my teammates as fun, hard-working *people*, not lesbians. But Jim was a traditional, macho kind of guy, who hadn't had the same exposure to lesbians as I had, and, in all fairness, he was exhibiting a commonplace reaction of the times. I imagined that over time, social attitudes toward gays and lesbians would change. Unfortunately the lesbian label was still strongly associated with women athletes.

I turned sideways and looked out the window at the passing barren corn fields. Finally, I spoke. "Well, I'm going to keep playing, regardless of whether you come to watch."

He looked straight ahead at the road. "I understand, and that's fine."

*****

Jim was a dedicated special education teacher. I watched him respond to his students with enormous kindness and patience. Students with cerebral palsy, Down syndrome, mental challenges, and assorted congenital conditions clamored to be at his side. He spoke to them with genuine affection, yet still maintained the discipline that was needed for such a diverse classroom. He was their teacher, advocate, and friend. One time I asked Jim what led him to special education.

"My brother Steve, of course," he admitted.

As a proponent for Special Olympics, Jim volunteered at various local and state contests. I accompanied him to several Special Olympics events, which exposed me to a new world of competition. Whereas I was used to seeing full-bodied, highly skilled athletes in competitions, it was fascinating to witness the competitiveness among the disabled athletes as they strove to do their best. There was equality, too---male, female, old, young, one arm, no legs, wheel-chair bound, mentally-challenged, blind. The invitation to compete was open to everyone, which was great to witness. As I mingled with these special athletes, I felt uncomfortable at times, mostly due to my ignorance and lack of exposure to the various mental and physical conditions. It made me more sensitive to Jim's uneasiness around my lesbian friends. Most of us are wary of that which we do not fully understand.

*****

Since both Jim and I liked sports, we would occasionally play various sports together. Whether it was bowling, tennis, golf, or Ping-Pong, these were the rare situations where conflicts arose in our relationship. Because of my fierce competitiveness, I played hard and tried to win. Even as an adult I enjoyed the physicality of sports and the potential for victory. Both were innate to my being. I thrived on both the physical and mental challenges inherent in sports. I was a gracious loser, but winning definitely trumped losing in my book. Being a traditional kind of guy, Jim was not used to getting beat by a female. Not that I always won, but when I did, he would get moody.

Jim and I decided to play tennis on an unusually mild day in late February. Indiana weather was unpredictable the latter part of winter. We might experience a blizzard, tornado, ice storm, or a warm spring-like day. This particular day was warmer than usual and people were outside biking, walking, and jogging. Mothers were pushing baby strollers along sidewalks. Once we got to the tennis courts and had hit back and forth for awhile, we decided to play a full match. I won the first set, 6-3. During the second set I noticed that Jim's otherwise sunny disposition was disintegrating toward displeasure. After a particularly long exchange of baseline shots and volleys, I eventually won the point. As I was walking back to the baseline to serve, a tennis ball whipped past my head so close that it brushed my ear. I turned abruptly and faced Jim, who was standing with his hands on his hips, a scowl covered his face.

"Did you just try to hit me?" I screamed at him.

Rather than respond to my question, he squatted down in a ready stance and commanded, "Serve it up!"

I stared across the net at him. My ensuing emotion created a blur of thoughts. *He just tried to hurt me....he's my boyfriend....why would he do that?....does he hate me?....by God, I'm gonna beat his ass!....maybe I should let up and give him a few points....why can't he appreciate my skill?....I feel sorry for him....why do guys always have to feel superior?*

I abandoned my natural competitiveness and deliberately double-faulted my serve to give him the next point. Recognizing that I rarely double-fault and was handing over a free point, Jim pulled a ball from his pocket and slammed it back to me with such ferocity that it frightened me.

"Don't patronize me!" he shouted.

"We're done," I yelled as I stomped toward the fence to grab my bag and water bottle. I continued walking briskly toward the car and Jim followed, cursing with every step. After each of us slammed closed our respective car doors, we sat in silence. Tears began filling my eyes. "Why can't you accept me as a good athlete?" I muttered.

Jim was gripping the steering wheel so hard that his knuckles were white. He slammed one hand against the dashboard. "Dammit, Debbie. Guys don't like being beaten by a girl!"

I reached down to kick off my tennis shoes. Every feminist cell in my body was activated. "You know what? I bet Chris Evert beats most of the guys that *she* dates!"

Jim pressed his lips together and turned to look at me. "But Chris Evert is not *my* girlfriend." His tone was coarse.

The same song that I had heard for years began playing in my head. The lyrics never changed: *Girls are to be quiet and good. Be subservient to boys. Don't get sweaty or dirty. Guys don't like a strong, independent woman. Let boys win or they won't like you.*

We drove back to my apartment in that disturbed silence that engulfs all couples during strife. I felt a piercing sort of pain in my heart. I slammed the car door and went inside alone while Jim drove off. I loved him and didn't want this conflict to persist. But this was the ongoing cultural dilemma that I continued to face, along with the young women who I coached and mentored. The message of sports has always been *"be aggressive....go for it....be intense."* The message of society, however, was *"be a lady....be submissive....be pretty."* Title IX had opened opportunities for women, but had not totally changed the culture. Whereas participation in athletics can enhance self-confidence and character in both men and women, it may take many more years for cultural norms to change to the point that women will no longer be afraid to do their best or be superior---in sports, in the classroom, and in the work place. As women we should be allowed to celebrate a full range of choices. Being an athlete doesn't mean we are rejecting or eliminating the nurturing and feminine aspects of who we are. But some men like Jim don't yet see us this way as balanced creatures.

Later that evening I called Jim and we talked for a long time. We both apologized, but I also told him that in close relationships, people crave acceptance---to be loved for being who they are.

"Like anyone else I have many flaws, but I don't view athleticism or competitiveness as one of them," I sobbed. "I can't pretend."

The sting from the afternoon was gone, but I knew it wasn't totally resolved. This would be something that we'd both have to work on in a society that was slow to change its perception and expectations of women.

*****

My Northside girls' basketball team lost in the sectional tournament, so our season was over by the first of March. I was proud nevertheless of the improvements the girls had made in their skills and understanding of basketball. As expected, we were all sorry that the season was over, but since loss always invites reflection, the girls promised to be better next year. Their sustained optimism and enthusiasm inspired me.

Because tennis season was more than a month away, I had a rare breather from coaching. Part of that breathing time was to be spent in Gallup, New Mexico, where my Marion-Kay Pepper team was to compete in the 1975 AAU National Basketball Championships. My competitive juices were reignited as we traveled to compete against the best women's teams in the country. Even though our team practiced together only once a week, we did well in the tournament, advancing to the Final Four. Unfortunately, we faced a superior team from Fullerton, California, and lost in the semi-finals. Interestingly the Wayland Hutcherson Flying Queens of Plainview, Texas, played in the other semifinal and eventually won the entire tournament. Harley Redin was no longer their coach, but seeing their fancy blue and gold uniforms brought back the painful memory of my "pseudo" Pan American Games tryout on the Wayland Baptist campus during my sophomore year in college.

One of the featured events during the AAU Nationals was the free throw shooting contest. Each team selected one player to represent their team in the competition. My teammates selected me. Preliminary rounds were conducted between games where each contestant shot twenty-five free throws. I performed well enough to make it to the final round where two players would vie for the title by simultaneously shooting free throws at opposite ends of the court. Whoever made the most shots out of fifty would be crowned the National Free Throw Champion. My opponent was a member of the Wayland Baptist team. About 300 spectators gathered in the bleachers to watch us shoot. Maxine Thayer, our grandmotherly manager, came to the court to rebound for me. Maxine was a short, rotund woman with gray hair and thick glasses. She always stood out in a crowd by wearing wildly-colored polyester pantsuits. As I took my place at the free throw line Maxine patted me on the back and handed me the ball. "Debbie, just do your thing," she whispered in my ear. She walked to the basket and stood directly under the net to retrieve my shots.

The crowd was hushed as my opponent and I began shooting. A scorekeeper seated at each end of the court kept a tally of made and missed shots. There was no time restriction. We merely shot at our own pace. Since my opponent and I had our backs to each other, there was no way for either of us to assess who was ahead as we continued shooting. The only indication of progress was the "oohs," "aahs," and sighs from the supporters. I made my first thirty shots without a miss. I could feel the tension and excitement building in the gym. Had my opponent made her first thirty? Was I ahead? I focused on maintaining a rhythm that was reminiscent of my hours of free throw shooting as a young girl on my driveway. The same routine had carried me through college basketball. *Right toe at the line...bent knees...bounce the ball three times...elbow under the ball...launch the ball with a high arc and a flick of the wrist.*

Fatigue was starting to set in and I could feel tightness building in my shoulders and upper back. A few of my shots bounced around on the rim but luckily fell through the net. Then one bounced out. I was thirty-nine out of forty. My heart was racing and I paused to take a few deep breaths. Maxine nodded her head and smiled. I read her lips.

"Only ten more," she mouthed to me.

Perspiration was dripping down my brow. I bent down and wiped my sweaty palms on the back my calf-high tube socks.

"Concentrate," I mumbled to myself. "Block out the crowd. Pretend you're all alone."

My arms felt shaky but I closed my eyes and visualized myself as a ten-year-old girl shooting free throws at the rickety backboard affixed to top of my garage. Dad was standing by my side, reminding me to relax and concentrate on the front of the rim.

Amid the cheers of my Marion-Kay Pepper teammates I made the next ten shots. I had made forty-nine out of fifty free throws. I turned and looked at the opposite end of the court to watch my opponent make her final four shots. I was unaware of the final tally, but my teammates knew the outcome because they had been keeping track. My opponent had missed three of her fifty shots, so I was the champion. I met my opponent at half-court and shook her hand. We both had the same bedraggled look as if we had just played an entire game---sweaty and spent. The director of the tournament handed me a large gold trophy. I breathed a sigh of relief as I held my trophy in the air and pumped it toward my teammates who were on their feet cheering. I was twenty-four years old and holding my very first individual trophy for sports. At the top of the trophy was a miniature bronze statue of a curvaceous female basketball player.

Marion-Kay Peppers (Debbie – just left of sign)

*****

Spring was finally upon us and I was coaching tennis. Tennis was not as intense for me to coach. Other than occasionally tweaking players' strokes and serves, it was more organizational than anything--- setting up challenges to determine who was #1, #2, and #3 in singles, and who teamed together well in doubles. During practices I had them work on drills and then play each other. It was great to be outside and enjoy the warm weather. Since this was my final season for coaching tennis, I tried to imagine the freedom that next spring would bring without a commitment to any sport.

My relationship with Jim was becoming more serious. We were spending much of our free time together. It was all good. We were in love. We spent spring break in San Diego, visiting my brother, Mike, who was now an anesthesiologist at Scripps Hospital. Away from the daily grind of teaching and coaching, Jim and I enjoyed leisurely walks, touring the city, dinners out, lounging on the beach, and the general feeling of having no teaching and coaching responsibilities. It gave us time to bond more deeply.

A week after we returned from San Diego, Jim was at my apartment watching a baseball game on television while I was at the grocery store buying food for dinner. When I returned I could tell by Jim's body language that something was bothering him. He barely looked at me as I entered the apartment and he had his arms crossed tightly across his chest. His brow was wrinkled and a scowl covered his face.

I set my grocery bag on the kitchen table. "What's wrong?" I asked.

He kept his eyes glued to the television screen. "You got a phone call while you were gone."

"Who was it?"

"Dallas Kunkle. He wanted to know if you could come over to the gym and play basketball with him and the guys. They need one more player." His voice seemed strained and he still didn't look at me.

"Okay, and what did you say?"

"I told him that you weren't here." He hesitated. "Then I asked if he wanted *me* to come play since you were gone."

"And?" I asked.

"He told me 'No, just have Debbie call when she gets home.'" I detected a hateful edge to Jim's voice.

A sudden surge of sadness hit me. Poor Jim, what a blow to his ego! Dallas's comment had to hurt. We had been working together to overcome the gender role situations that caused occasional conflicts. Jim had become more understanding of my competitive, independent nature, and I was more sensitive to his feelings.

"I'm so sorry, Jim. I'll call Dallas back and tell him I can't make it."

Jim stood up and walked to the refrigerator and opened a beer. "No. Go play basketball with the guys. And *I'll* stay here and fix dinner for us!" The sarcasm in his voice cut me like a blade.

"Jim, all I can say is that I'm sorry. I know how hard that was to take."

"Yeah, I'm the only guy I know whose girlfriend is summoned to play sports over him!"

I put my arms around him and laid my head on his shoulder. At first he kept his arms stiffly at his side, but finally responded and hugged me tightly. I rubbed his back and he stroked my hair. We kissed deeply.

I interrupted our embrace. "You're a good man, Jim Powers," I whispered into his ear.

At the end of the school year, Jim asked me to marry him. Without hesitation I said "yes."

CHAPTER 15

THE 1975 VOLLEYBALL TEAM

I spent the summer of 1975 completing my master's degree at Ball State. Jim was busy directing camp activities at Camp Isanogel. I enjoyed sitting around the camp pool working on my thesis and watching Jim interact so lovingly with the campers. He would lower them gently into the pool, their contorted limbs dangling. They were so frail. Wheelchairs and leg braces surrounded the pool, but giggles and screeches of delight filled the sun-bleached air. I helped Jim rearrange the dining hall for camp socials, and danced to the beat of the Rolling Stones and Fleetwood Mac with campers afflicted with cerebral palsy, muscular dystrophy, and blindness. How blessed I felt to be able-bodied.

One evening while relaxing in his cabin, I asked Jim if he had selected an engagement ring for me.

His eyes widened when he looked at me. "Really? You want an engagement ring?" he asked with a quizzical look on his face.

I sat up straight and stared at him. "You're kidding me. I know I'm not a "girlie" girl, but *every* girl wants a ring! You mean you weren't planning on surprising me with one?"

He pulled me close and pulled playfully at my ring finger. "Then a ring you shall have. We'll go shopping together for one."

I shook my head in amazement and giggled. "Jeez, Jim, your romanticism overwhelms me."

"It's certainly not one of my strongest traits," he lamented.

"Luckily I'm not a chocolates-and-flowers kind of girl. And, by the way, I love ALL of your traits, Jim."

As the summer vacation wound down, we decided to get married in December so we could take advantage of the school's holiday break for a week's honeymoon and additional time to settle into the small house we had found to rent. I approached the new school year with extra vigor and excitement. Fall would bring an exciting volleyball season in which my team would be defending state champions, *and* I had a wedding to plan. I contacted the Marion-Kay Peppers and told them that I would not be playing on their team this winter. Unfortunately the *Indianapolis Star* had just run a feature story on me as the star of the Peppers and defending national free throw champion. I had also recently been named Indiana's 1974 outstanding AAU basketball player. It wasn't easy for me to say farewell to this important part of my life. Playing basketball had been the love of my twenty-four-year-old existence. But now I was exchanging my basketball sneakers for wedding slippers, and I was discovering that my new role as a coach fueled much of my competitive fire. I had definitely cultivated an addiction to my new pursuit.

The announcement of our engagement created a buzz around school. Teaching colleagues congratulated us, and my students and athletes clamored around me wanting details. Janie Wierks, my co-teacher in physical education, had moved away during the summer to take a new job. Her replacement was a former classmate and teammate of mine at Indiana University. Though not a starter, Donna Palivec was an undergraduate member of the basketball team during my senior season. She was a great person and a strong physical educator. I looked forward to working with her at Northside. She would be taking over the swimming and track and field coaching duties as well as teaching physical education along with me. Because the girls' sports program was expanding and becoming more competitive, Mr. Lemna hired a local woman to coach gymnastics and tennis. Softball had been added to the offerings, and our athletic director, Mr. Carmichael, chose to be their coach. The boys' golf coach volunteered to start a girls' golf team. A female teacher whose daughter was a cheerleader volunteered to take over the cheerleaders. As expected, Title IX was slowly providing female athletes with more opportunities. Money was still very tight and sharing facilities was an ongoing problem. Boys' basketball and football still ruled the roost because they brought in the largest crowds.

Because teaching and coaching had devoured many of my waking hours over the past two years, I had lost contact with the developments in women's sports at Indiana University. Since Donna was a recent graduate, she informed me that the women athletes were now receiving scholarships, had access to training facilities, traveled on charter buses, and played expanded schedules. I couldn't help but feel pangs of envy as she described their Big Ten conference schedule, game and practice facilities, uniforms, All-American distinctions, and travel budget. When I was on the team, we had been coached by part-time graduate students. Donna told me that they now had full-time coaches and assistants. Times were definitely changing.

The biggest news of the time was that the 1976 Summer Olympics would be offering women's basketball competition for the first time. The U.S. team was being selected from the ranks of current college players. Once again I felt a surge of jealousy. When I had been a college player, the U.S. Pan American Games national team was selected from AAU players. And now that I was an AAU player, the national team was being selected from college players! I had been at the wrong stages to achieve my childhood dream of being an Olympian! Nevertheless, I was happy that women's basketball was finally earning recognition as an Olympic sport.

*****

With the commencement of the new school year it was time to concentrate on volleyball. Five seniors had graduated from my eleven-member 1974 state championship volleyball team, which would mean bringing several players up to varsity from last year's junior varsity team. They would have to gel quickly. It would take a lot of hard work and commitment over the next three months to be ready to defend our state title in November. I was counting on the six returning players to assume a strong leadership role and be models of dedication to these new players.

- Kasey was my returning starting setter. Now a senior, she was one of the most gifted athletes I had ever seen. Not only was she a terrific volleyball player, but she had won an individual swimming state championship and gone to the state finals in track and field. There was not one sport in which she did not excel. She was also a cheerleader and one of the cutest girls in the school. Kasey was the object of attention of many of the boys at Northside, with her blonde pixie haircut, twinkling aquamarine eyes, and dazzling smile. She had a very sweet demeanor, almost to the point of naiveté. I was pretty confident that Kasey could date any boy she wanted. Her current boyfriend was a handsome, popular athlete at the school.

- Sallie was my top returning hitter. While only 5'7" tall, she had powerful legs that resulted in a huge vertical jump. Sallie was also a gifted athlete, being a two-time state champion in track.

- Liz was a quiet leader who was a backcourt passing specialist. Very few spikes from opposing players hit the floor if they were directed anywhere close to her. She would dive everywhere to pick up hard-driven hits. Even though she was short, she also played the front row. She was a deceptive spiker.

- Annie was the tallest player on the team at 5'8" and another strong hitter. Also a senior and a cheerleader, she was the jokester, always keeping the mood light.

- Jill was our serving specialist. Her bomber serves struck fear in opponents' eyes. Jill had a tendency to get down on herself. So, as long as I could keep her confidence at a high level, Jill could be counted on for several service aces in each match.

- Mel was my little freshman who confidently served the winning point at last season's state championship match. As an experienced sophomore I expected her to assume a stronger role on the team. Shy and slightly built, she had a smile that could light up a room. Her enthusiasm and competitiveness were contagious.

- Susie was our returning manager. She was an exceptionally mature senior who was efficient and reliable. She had puppy-dog brown eyes and an infectious smile. I had cut her from the team the previous year during tryouts, but admired her spirit and enthusiasm so much that I chose her to be our manager. It didn't hurt that she often showed up at practice with a plate of freshly baked chocolate chip cookies. Everyone on the team loved Susie. She was like a big sister to them, and her demeanor provided a calming effect on everyone, including me. She had been the perfect manager for us.

These six returning players and senior manager would be the solid core, supported by a new cast of players who had sat in the bleachers at last year's state championship hopefully feeling a flame of urgency to be on the team and help win it all again this year.

I carefully selected the new players to complete the roster. Shelley had been a capable setter on the junior varsity. Though now a senior, I needed her to provide back-up to Kasey. We had lost a setter from last year's team to graduation, leaving Kasey as my only experienced setter. As director of the offense, the setter is unquestionably the most important player on a volleyball team. She runs around the court chasing the passed balls from the backcourt players and must convert them to a high set to one of the front-row hitters. She must be quick and agile with good, soft setting hands. My challenge with Shelley would be to keep her motivated and happy as a senior sitting on the bench most of the time since Kasey was our number one setter.

I moved four other players up from the junior varsity to complete the roster in areas where players had graduated---another hitter and back-row defensive specialists. Eight seniors, one junior, and two sophomores made up the new team. I worried that we were not very tall. No one was over 5'8", which meant we would have to be an impenetrable defensive team. I selected Kasey and Annie as co-captains and told them that their leadership was a key to keeping the team focused.

"We won't let you down, coach," they chimed together when I told them their role.

The season started strong, with several easy victories. Even though we had lost five players from last year's team, we were still viewed as defending state champions and the team to beat. I constantly warned the girls that there would be no easy contest. There would be a target on our backs at every match.

Whereas victories will enshrine a team, adversity can define it. Several weeks after the start of our season, Mr. Lemna called me into his office. My tennis shoes squeaked on the freshly polished linoleum as I approached his desk. (I always thought I was the luckiest female teacher in the building, permitted to wear comfortable tennis shoes all day.) After I sat down Mr. Lemna took a long drink of coffee and cleared his throat. Before speaking he picked up a pencil and began tapping it rhythmically on his desk.

"We have a situation," he stated.

I searched his face for clues as to the nature of this "situation." By his mannerisms and tone I had a feeling that it was not a good situation.

"It is rumored that one of your volleyball players is involved in an inappropriate relationship with a married male teacher in the school."

I blinked my eyes several times and then opened them wide and stared at him. I was speechless.

"I take it from your reaction that you know nothing about this?" he asked.

"Mr. Lemna, I am shocked and totally unaware of anything like that going on." I hesitated before continuing. "Which one of my athletes?"

"Kasey," he responded. "And the teacher is Coach Harper."

"Kasey, my star player and captain?" I exclaimed. "I can't believe it!"

Mr. Lemna leaned back in his chair and ran his fingers through his curly hair. "I would like for you to do some investigating. As soon as possible, call Kasey in and talk to her. See what you can find out. Then search her gym locker to see if you find any notes or letters to her from Coach Harper. We need evidence to know if this is indeed happening. This is very serious."

I rose slowly from my chair. My head was now filled with a fog of disbelief and anger. "I'll talk to her tonight after practice."

"One more thing," Mr. Lemna said. I sat back down.

Mr. Lemna cleared his throat again and paused. "There is a rule in our school system that a married couple cannot teach in the same building, so either you or Jim will not be able to teach at Northside next year once you are married. However, you can both finish this current school year that ends in June."

My mouth dropped open and my hands gripped the arms of my chair. "You're kidding," I stammered.

I could tell Mr. Lemna was uncomfortable with the double whammy he had just given me---my best player involved with a teacher, and either Jim or I having to look for a new job next year. Mr. Lemna continued tapping his pencil and his jaw was clenched. He lowered his head and stared at his desk.

"I'm sorry," he said softly. "You are both outstanding teachers and I hate to lose either of you."

I stood abruptly and quickly collected my thoughts. "And I just won this school a state championship!" I shouted back to him. "Would you release the boys' basketball coach if he had just won a state title?" My cheeks blushed as I realized the brash content of my spontaneous outburst.

Mr. Lemna stood and spoke in a near whisper, ignoring my question, "I'm sorry. It's the rule. He walked over and opened the office door for me. "Let me know what you find out about Kasey."

The shrill of the passing bell filled the hallway as I stepped into the mass of students changing classes. The sound of banging metal lockers and the hum of teenagers' conversations echoed in my ears. I sidestepped students as I made my way toward the gymnasium in a haze of discontent.

"Good luck this weekend, Miss Millbern," I heard a student yell. I turned to see Dave, the leader of our boys' cheerblock. I waved back to him hoping he didn't notice the rage that was slowly engulfing me.

I sat in my office, adjacent to the girls' locker room in a stupor. I thought back to the times I had observed Coach Harper, Kasey, Annie, and a few other students playing one-wall handball in the gym during the lunch hour. During the lunch hour the gym was open for basketball, handball, and Ping Pong. It wasn't unusual for teachers to join in the games with students. I had done so several times. I had never noticed any unusual or inappropriate behavior between Coach Harper and Kasey.

Percy Harper was in his late thirties, a large man with well-defined musculature. The veins in his massive arms protruded like vines clinging to a tree trunk. He was one of the boys' physical education teachers and the head soccer coach. Because I found him to be arrogant and distant, I never liked him from the moment we met. With his bushy mustache and elongated sideburns, he gave me the impression that he was trying to be "cool" among the high school students. I wasn't impressed. Instead, I detected a hint of lechery in his eyes that made me feel uncomfortable. How could Kasey get caught up in a relationship with him? She already had a steady high school boyfriend! I couldn't help but reflect on my first-year teaching dilemma when senior athlete Brad Michaels had tried to seduce me at my apartment. Percy Harper had to be insane to pursue Kasey. Encouraging or concealing a teacher/student romance would be professional suicide!

My thoughts swirled back to problem number two: I might lose my job because of my marital status. How archaic! Wasn't it the covered-wagon-days when it was illegal for the one-room female school teachers to get married? How could a modern-day school system have such an equally antiquated rule? How could a married couple present a problem for a school? What a perplexing state of sexual mores I was confronted with in a single meeting with my principal. Jim and I would have a lot to discuss this evening over dinner.

Volleyball practice that afternoon was spirited and competitive. I loved the way the girls challenged each other to work harder. I tried to stay focused even after mentioning to Kasey at a water break that I needed to talk with her after practice in my office. She nodded and didn't seem to question the meeting. After all, it was not uncommon for me to meet with my captains one-on-one throughout the season. I gave Shelley some extra setting time during practice since I wasn't sure if Kasey would be suspended from the team if her indiscretion resulted in a suspension.

"How are things going?" I asked Kasey as she settled into the overstuffed chair adjacent to my desk after practice. She wiped the perspiration from her forehead with a towel and grinned at me.

"Fine," she responded. Her eyes appeared a deeper shade of blue in contrast to her flushed cheeks from the hard sprints I had them run at the end of practice. Perspiration continued to drip down the side of her face.

I searched for words to continue our conversation. Kasey was never very talkative, so I knew it would be a struggle.

"How do you think the team's coming together this year?" I asked.

"Good," she replied.

"Everything fine with your classes?"

"Yep."

The conversation was becoming more difficult. Kasey's one-word responses revealed nothing.

"I see you and Donnie are still dating." Kasey glanced at me with a quizzical look. I knew I was stepping into shaky territory.

Kasey looked down at the towel she was twisting in her hands. "Uh huh," she replied.

"Kasey, is there anything you want to share with me? Anything bothering you?"

Continuing to look down at the towel, Kasey's face became redder. Her body seemed to stiffen. I searched her face for the slightest sign of anything---fear, remorse, sadness, confusion.

"Nope."

I paused, searching for words to say. "Well you know that if you ever want to talk about anything, you can come to me," I reassured her, even though my intuition told me that she would never confide in me.

"Anything else?" she muttered.

I pointed toward the locker room. "No. Go ahead and get changed before you get chilled. Good practice today."

"Thanks," she said as she scurried out the door.

I leaned back in my chair and clasped my hands on top of my head. *Well, that went real well,* I sighed as I closed my eyes. Kasey seemed so innocent, so naïve. I hoped she hadn't been coerced into something that had put her way over her head. However, my intuition told me that her partial silence with me was a subtle form of lying.

After the locker room had cleared I walked through and picked up stray socks, towels, and hair brushes. I slowly approached Kasey's locker. Using the master key, I opened it. Volleyball sneakers, a mirror, a crumpled cheerleading skirt, sweaty socks, and a makeup bag were stacked in layers. I unzipped the makeup bag and gasped when I saw a neatly folded piece of paper with "To Kasey" written on the exposed side. As I carefully began to unfold the note, my eyes caught the signature at the very bottom of the page…..."Love, Coach H." My heart was pounding. I couldn't bear to read any more so I closed her locker and put the re-folded note in the top drawer of my desk. I would give it to Mr. Lemna the following morning.

At dinner Jim listened quietly as I told him about my meeting with Mr. Lemna about our future and the situation with Kasey. Like me, he was upset and surprised that there was a marriage rule.

"This is 1975, not 1875!" he muttered.

We decided to not let this ruin our school year or upcoming wedding.

"Something will work out," he assured me. As to Kasey, he told me that it was out of my control. "Let the administration handle it."

The next day was a Friday. I took the note to Mr. Lemna as soon as I arrived at school. I told him I had met with Kasey and she had not revealed anything about a relationship with Coach Harper, but I had found the note in her locker.

"I didn't read the contents, but I could see that it was from Coach Harper," I said.

Mr. Lemna placed the note in his pocket and told me that he would take care of it.

"Most likely nothing will happen until next week, after I've had a chance to meet with other school officials and the parties involved."

The weekend turned out to be the final blowup. Kasey had told her parents that she was spending the night with a girlfriend. Kasey's younger sister happened to run into this girlfriend while shopping at the mall that evening. When her sister asked where Kasey was, the girlfriend revealed that Kasey never intended to spend the night at her house. Instead, Kasey had gone to Indianapolis with Coach Harper. Apparently when Kasey's father learned of the charade, he immediately drove to Indianapolis and found Kasey with Coach Harper at a restaurant. Kasey's dad was livid and even threatened to kill the coach. I didn't learn about this tangled scenario until Monday, when the entire school was abuzz about it.

As should have happened, Coach Harper was suspended and, after an investigation, fired from his teaching and coaching job. Kasey was not punished by the school, but I knew that it would have an impact on her psyche and the team's cohesiveness. She was our captain, our leader! I anticipated that the secrecy and concealment would take its toll. After all, once exposed, the entire school knew about the affair, and Kasey faced her classmates shrouded with embarrassment. This was the type of distraction that we didn't need heading into the heart of our season. Even though I was irritated and disappointed at Kasey's indiscretion, I didn't want to ostracize or condemn her. I felt bad for her, deducing that she had gotten caught up in the flattery from a dominant adult man, and it had spiraled out of control.

When we commenced practices, I detected a mood of disgust toward Kasey among some of the players, but I hoped it would wear off as we got down to the business of winning volleyball matches. I didn't dare add to the tumult on the team by sharing my secret concern about losing my job. It was constantly on my mind that this might be my last year coaching these great kids, but I wasn't about to share my worry with them.

On the Saturday following Kasey's unfortunate fiasco we played in a four-team invitational tournament. We faced the host school, Wes-Del High School, in the first match of the morning. We won the first game easily, 15-0. Then, in front of my eyes, the team suddenly fell apart. The players stopped communicating and lost the continuity and selflessness that defines teamwork. They started bickering among themselves. I used all my time-outs to try to pull them together. I rearranged our rotation, substituting some of the eager, less-experienced players into the match for several of the veteran starters. Nothing seemed to work. Since the setter is the floor general, I finally substituted Shelley in for Kasey at setter, thinking that the girls might still be aggravated at Kasey. Kasey sat next to me on the bench, stooped over with her face in her hands. Her demeanor angered me. "Sit up, Kasey, and give Shelley your vocal support!" I commanded. "Be a leader!"

We lost the next two games 5-15 and 13-15, and thus lost the match. This was our first loss in two years---since my first year of coaching volleyball. Because most everyone in the packed gym except our fans was cheering against us, Wes-Del's victory created bedlam as their supporters rushed the floor. As the girls retreated to the locker room and slumped onto the benches with their heads hanging low, I felt their misery. *Our* misery! The impact of the past week's events reflected in our play, and I was as responsible as they were. I had failed to reconstitute my team from their encounter with a major distraction. Or was *I* the one who was distracted?

"Loss hurts," I spoke softly to the girls. "It bleeds and aches. This loss will follow you home and call out your name in the middle of the night. But it also invites reflection. Teams all season will be gunning for you. They want you to lose. But you are not losers. *We* are not losers. By Monday's practice, this loss should be a distant memory. By Monday's practice, last week's distraction should be a distant memory. Monday we start practicing *together* to win a second state championship!"

The girls rose slowly from their benches and huddled together. I retreated to the far edge of the room, leaving them alone. I could hear muffled talking, but couldn't tell what was said or who was saying it. Finally they gathered their hands in the middle and counted…"1, 2, 3…TEAM!" they shouted, raising their arms together. I hoped that they meant it---team. What they didn't understand is that one of the secrets of sports competition is that you can learn more from losing than winning. I had already learned that hard lesson over the years, and these girls were getting their first taste.

CHAPTER 16

MORE CHALLENGES

The burden of deciding how to handle next year's job uncertainty weighed heavily on Jim's and my minds. We went back and forth ......

"You stay at Northside."

"No, *you* stay."

"But you're a state championship coach."

"But your special needs students need continuity."

It still made me angry that one of us had to leave. Mr. Lemna was leaving the decision up to us, since he was confident that either teaching position could be filled. I was so busy coaching, teaching, and planning our wedding that I tried to block next year out of my mind. After the wedding, we could concentrate more on our future.

Since Mom and Dad lived in Miami, Florida, and we were getting married in Muncie, I was basically on my own making wedding arrangements. I talked to Mom often on the phone to ask her advice, but she would not be coming up until the week before the wedding to assist with last-minute preparations. Jim was a huge help. During our precious free time from school, we worked together on the guest list, invitations, rehearsal dinner, catering arrangements, honeymoon locations, tuxedoes and dresses for our attendants, and photographers. At least the church would already be beautifully decorated with holiday poinsettias for our December 20 event. That made the flower arrangements easy.

My volleyball team had rebounded from our tournament loss and was back in winning form. Kasey was setting the ball with pinpoint accuracy and hustling all over the court quicker than ever, most likely relieved of the secret burden she had been carrying. She finally admitted to me that she was glad to have been exposed, because the situation had gotten out of control. She had felt trapped and was very scared. "What was I thinking?" were her words of regret to me. Neither I nor anyone on the team ever discussed it again. Just like shaking off our loss, we had healed as a group from Kasey's trauma. It reminded me that one of the many benefits of being on a team is the opportunity to provide safety and comfort to a hurting member. Teams can become sanctuaries for healing. Both boys *and* girls are entitled to this opportunity for camaraderie and peer support through sports participation.

I sensed the team had a new drive, a new will, as sectional play was only a few weeks away. Sallie and Annie were spiking the ball as hard as bullets, and Mel, Liz, and Jill were black and blue from sprawling all over the court digging hard-driven spikes. The new players were performing like seasoned veterans, substituting into games to serve a timely ace or get a key block or dig.

The boys' cheerblock was growing. Football and basketball players, class officers, and the most popular boys in the school rushed into every match vying for front row seats in the block. They developed rousing cheers for both offensive and defensive aspects of the game. Their most beloved chant, the one most motivating to my team, was what we heard moments before running onto the court to start a match: **"Millbern, Millbern open the door. Let those Titans on the floor!"** The boys would chant this repeatedly with increasing volume just before we jogged out of the locker room. To witness the passion these boys had for a girls' team was beyond anything I had ever experienced or expected.

Three weeks before sectionals I received a late night telephone call from another female volleyball coach in a nearby town. We had played her team several times over the past seasons and I considered her a friend.

"Have you heard about the boys playing volleyball?" she asked.

"What do you mean?" I had no idea what she was talking about.

"There is a girls' team up in South Bend that has two boys playing on their team."

"What? You're kidding!" I gasped.

She continued. "South Bend Clay High School is allowing two guys, two *big* guys, to play on their girls' volleyball team. I guess they're creaming everyone!"

I pulled the phone earpiece away from my ear and looked at it as if it was lying to me or I was not hearing the words correctly. "How can that be legal?" I asked.

"Don't know," she responded. "But you'll probably face them at state. And, guess what, their coach is a woman! Joan Mitchell! Can you believe she would be such a traitor to girls' sports?"

She hung up and I looked at the clock. Too late to call Mr. Lemna or Mr. Carmichael. I'd have to wait until tomorrow to learn if this is true or merely a temporary chauvinistic prank by some high school boys. I didn't know Joan Mitchell. *Guys on a girls' team? How can that be?* I thought.

The next day, after a discussion with Mr. Lemna and a subsequent call to the Indiana High School Athletic Association (IHSAA) office in Indianapolis, the rumor was verified. Two boys were indeed playing on Clay's girls' volleyball team. The IHSAA staff member explained the developing scenario to us: Just after the passage of Title IX in 1972, many schools could not immediately fund girls' teams. Therefore, a father of an Indiana high school female golfer had petitioned the IHSAA to allow his daughter to play on the *boys'* golf team since her school did not offer girls' golf. The IHSAA denied his petition, prompting the father to sue the IHSAA for discrimination. The lawsuit traveled all the way to the Indiana Supreme Court where the father won. The court upheld the "equal opportunity" interpretation of Title IX. Thus, the girl was allowed to play on her high school boys' golf team, and the court forced the IHSAA to pass a rule stating that *"girls could play on boys' non-contact sports teams if their school did not offer that same sport for girls."* This was hoped to be a short-lived rule once schools were able to expand more sports offerings for girls. In the meantime, girls were popping up occasionally on boys' golf, tennis, baseball, and swim teams.

Since the IHSAA rule did not address the opposite scenario, of boys playing on *girls'* teams, two South Bend Clay boys had decided this season to play on their girls' volleyball team since their high school did not offer boys' volleyball. One of the boys' fathers was an attorney who was adamant about his son's opportunity to play. His son, Brian Goralski, was an outstanding 6'3" player who had been on the boys' U.S. Junior Olympic Volleyball Team. His dad had hopes of Brian earning a scholarship on a men's collegiate volleyball team. Therefore, he and his son were looking for opportunities to showcase Brian's talent. Also, they wanted to make a statement to the IHSAA about the need for boys' volleyball to become a sanctioned high school sport in the state. Some states had already sanctioned boys' high school volleyball and conducted state tournaments, but Indiana was not one of them. At several colleges and universities, men's volleyball was a popular NCAA-sanctioned sport. Schools like UCLA, Ball State, Ohio State, Pepperdine, Long Beach State, and others played volleyball at a very high level, and athletic scholarships were awarded to high school boys who wanted to play in college.

Apparently Brian had talked another boy at his school, Ed Derse, into joining him on the girls' team. Even though the two female members on the IHSAA executive board disagreed with the boys inclusion on a girls' team, the IHSAA commissioner, Phil Eskew, stated that because the Indiana Supreme Court ruling gave girls the opportunity to play on boys' teams, "It stands to reason that the vice versa is true, too."

Hearing the chain of events made my blood boil. Yes, volleyball was a non-contact sport, but the ball can become a sixty-mile-per-hour projectile across the net if launched from the swift arm of a tall, muscular guy. Plus, the boys would be playing on the lower girls' net height of 7'4", compared to all-boys high school teams who compete on a 7'11" net. A girl playing on a boys' golf team is one thing. A 6'3" guy smashing balls at 5'6" girls is something else. Where is the justice in that? After years of sitting on the sidelines, women had finally earned the right to play high school sports. We finally had a state championship title for which to strive. I reflected on all the years I sat in the bleachers watching boys play because I was prohibited from trying out for their teams. Title IX changed all that. Now it was backfiring due to a frail interpretation. How dare two high school boys deny two female spots on their school's team! How dare that coach let them play! How dare they invade our new arena of opportunity! Those athletically-talented boys could probably play basketball, soccer, baseball, football, or a multitude of sports that they had been privileged to play since they were little boys. Why occupy *our* fledgling sport? If Brian Goralski was a junior Olympian, he had already showcased his talents to collegiate volleyball coaches. And what challenge or thrill would it be for these boys to beat teams of girls who were physically smaller and weaker? I thought about Northside High School, where our boy athletes proudly formed a cheerblock to celebrate our girls' athletic talents. They didn't try to play on our girls' teams! I was steaming with resentment.

I had more questions than answers as I stewed about what my team could possibly face if we made it to the state tournament. Since word would spread quickly to my team about the possibility of playing Brian's team at the state tournament, I decided the best angle would be to downplay his abilities to them and emphasize how much our skill and finesse could override his strength. I was actually lying through my teeth, because I knew how one or two exceptional players could dominate a volleyball match---female *or* male. Thankfully, when I explained the situation to the girls, I was relieved to see them nonchalantly nod their heads, brimming with their normal confidence.

"I refuse to define ourselves as victims," I told them. "And besides, we need to win sectionals and regionals to even have a chance to play South Bend Clay. Let's concentrate on that." Finally I added, "Just remember, Billie Jean King beat Bobby Riggs."

Still, I tried to imagine what the South Bend Clay school atmosphere was like for Brian and Ed, their female teammates, the female coach, and the other guys in their school. Wouldn't there be a lot of teasing and heckling from opponents? How did the girls' parents react to boys playing on a team with their daughters? What would the team chemistry be like on a male-dominated girls' team? Would the coach be ridiculed by feminists? Wouldn't some of the guys at Clay High School tease Brian and Ed? Since South Bend was so far away from Muncie, and since girls' sports were rarely covered in newspapers, I had no insight into how the South Bend community was handling the situation, or if there had even been much publicity. The less publicity, the better, I concluded. My job was to keep my girls focused on our goal.

We were 18-1 as we entered tournament play. At the sectionals we avenged our season's only loss by defeating Wes-Del in the first round, then downing Burris and Delta High Schools to earn our third straight sectional championship. Next up was regionals.

A few days before regionals Mr. Carmichael stopped by the gym while we were practicing. The pounding of spiked balls hitting the floor, sneakers squeaking on the shiny wood, and groans of effort echoed in the gym as he trudged across the floor lugging an oversized cardboard box. The loud thud of his box hitting the floor halted our play.

A grin formed on Mr. Carmichael's face and his eyes glistened. "Everyone come on over and see what's in this box."

Without hesitating, the girls and I jogged over and stood in front of him. The girls looked quizzically at me. My surprised expression signaled that I was in the dark as much as they were about what was in the box.

Mr. Carmichael cleared his throat and glanced at each of us. "This team has distinguished itself beyond anything we could have imagined. Miss Millbern, in your three years here at Northside your record of 58 wins and 3 losses is exemplary. Girls, your athleticism, dedication, and sportsmanship have resulted in several letters of praise coming into my office from around the state."

Mr. Carmichael leaned down and carefully pulled up a flap on the box. The girls shuffled forward and leaned over the box for a glimpse. Perspiration dripped from their faces onto the box, creating a collage of wet polka dots. Reaching inside the box Mr. Carmichael pulled out bundles of blue and red polyester warm-ups. He began tossing the pants and jackets to the girls. They were navy blue with red and white trim. When the team realized what they were getting, shrieks of joy filled the gym. The girls hugged their precious gifts to their chests and began crying and prancing around the gym. Several girls fell to the floor and began frantically tugging on the pants. Others pulled the jackets over their sweaty T-shirts. The joy in their faces brought tears to my eyes. Mr. Carmichael beamed as I hugged him.

"Thank you," I whispered in his ear.

"You are more than welcome." He stepped back, placed his hands on his hips, and chuckled as he watched the pandemonium unfolding in front of him. "Lordy, I've never seen any of the boys' teams get this excited when I gave them new warm-ups!"

"That's because these girls don't feel entitled. They appreciate anything they receive and any recognition they get. They play for the pure love of the sport."

As the team was loading the bus for the regional tournament several of the girls' parents approached me. The parents had become very dear to me. They had been an unfailing source of encouragement to their daughters and me all season. I was especially happy to see how the dads reacted to their daughters' athleticism and toughness. They exhibited what I saw in my own father as he treated me with admiration and respect as a young female athlete. As more girls begin playing organized sports in the future, I anticipated that there would be increasing parental interest in both sons' *and* daughters' athletic experiences within families.

Sallie's mother gently touched my arm as we stood on the curb watching the girls climb the steps onto the bus. "Did you know that all of the girls slept in their new warm-ups last night?"

"You're kidding!" I laughed as I noticed the other parents nodding their heads in agreement.

"They were so excited to get them," Kasey's dad chimed in. "In fact, I don't think Kasey's taken hers off since she brought it home!"

I turned to face the parents. "Your daughters' drive and determination is so refreshing." I paused as I felt a lump forming in my throat, struggling to find the right words. "Thank you for having such amazing daughters, and thank you for allowing me to coach them. It has been such a privilege."

Mel's mom stepped forward. "Thank *you* for being their coach. You know they'd do anything for you because they really look up to you. You're a wonderful role model." I saw several parents nod their heads in agreement, and a sensation of satisfaction penetrated my soul. I hugged Mel's mom and several of the other parents. *This coaching gig is special*, I thought to myself, *really special*. Somehow I didn't feel like I was wasting my life like my high school chemistry teacher had forecasted when I had proudly told him that I wanted to be a physical educator.

*****

The regional tournament proved to be the most challenging experience I had faced in my coaching career when an unsettling incident occurred in the final match. After tallying an easy win in the morning match, we found ourselves engaged in a hotly contested match against Carmel High School. A trip to the state championship was on the line. Our boys' cheerblock was exceptionally loud and rowdy. The gym resonated with their chants and cheers as my girls took the floor. Carmel had a good team. Their setter was a stunningly attractive girl with long blonde hair. In their teenage exuberance, our boys' cheerblock targeted this girl and began shouting her name whenever she touched the ball. Obviously trying to rattle her, they whistled at her and yelled questions to her.

"Do you have a boyfriend?"... *"Can I have a date?"* ... *"Nice legs!"* were a few of the statements I heard. I thought the guys were being pretty harsh, but my girls had faced similar taunts from opposing fans throughout the season, and I had coached them to be oblivious to such comments. I had trained my girls to focus on the game. We won the first game 15-8 and were leading the second game 6-0 when a strange turn of events caught us off guard.

During the middle of a long rally, the female referee blew her whistle to stop the play and signaled a point for Carmel. I jumped up off the bench and sent our floor captain, Kasey, over to the referee to question the call. The referee ignored Kasey and simply shouted toward me and our bench, "Point for Carmel due to unsportsmanlike conduct."

Since I had never heard of such a call, I extended my palms upward, shrugged my shoulders, and gave her a look of disbelief. She immediately signaled play to begin and Kasey dashed back to her setting position. Again, while the ball was being played back and forth over the net, the shrill of the referee's whistle halted the action. Holding her index finger in the air she shouted, "Point for Carmel due to unsportsmanlike conduct."

At this point I exploded off the bench and stomped to the sideline. Our fans were booing and jeering at the referee. My team looked at me with expressions of bewilderment. Since I hadn't seen any sign of unsportsmanlike behavior from my team, I asked the referee for permission to address her. She nodded and our fans clapped loudly as I walked across the court to talk to her. She leaned down from her tower above the net. I estimated her to be in late fifties. Her appearance and demeanor reminded me of some of my old physical education professors at Indiana University. Her short-cropped salt and pepper hair shone under the bright gym lights. I noticed beads of perspiration on her forehead.

"What's the problem?" I asked.

"I am penalizing your team because your boys' cheerblock is too loud."

I shook my head in disbelief. "You're kidding," I said with a hint of amusement in my voice.

"They need to be quiet when Carmel is serving," she retorted.

I placed my hands on my hips and stared at her. "Where in the rulebook does it state that the crowd has to be silent during the serve?" From the corner of my eye I saw Mr. Lemna and Mr. Carmichael descending the bleachers from their seats near the top of the gym.

Ignoring my question, she waved her hand toward the boys' cheerblock. "You need to calm them down."

"May I talk to them?" I asked.

"Yes, but make it quick or I'll penalize you for 'delay of game'."

I walked quickly toward our block of fans. By this time Mr. Lemna and Mr. Carmichael were on the floor beside me.

Looking over the huge block of fans in front of me, I shouted at the top of my voice, "The referee says that you guys need to calm down and not yell at the Carmel players when they're trying to serve!" I had difficulty concealing the smirk on my face as I spoke.

The boys started laughing and slapping each other on their backs while I looked nervously back at the referee. She was wiping her face with a towel.

"Please, guys, cooperate. We could lose this match!"

Neither Mr. Lemna nor Mr. Carmichael said anything, but had concerned looks on their faces. After hearing my plea they sat down next to our boys' block on the front row.

I hurried back to our bench. "Just play," I told the girls. "It's nothing you've done. Let's finish this match before it gets more out of control."

As Carmel served the ball, our fans were deathly silent, but as soon as the ball came back to their side, a few of the guys blurted out the word *"sissy"* when their blonde setter touched the ball. A whistle immediately interrupted play.

"Point, Carmel," the referee shouted.

Frustration and anger were now swallowing me. Carmel's setter, obviously rattled, covered her face with her hands and was starting to cry.

"Oh, brother," I muttered as I peered down the bench at Carmel's coach. She was merely clapping, celebrating another unearned point. I quickly called a time-out and walked over to the referee once again.

I pointed my finger at her and tried to speak calmly. "You know, if you can't handle competitive enthusiasm from fans, you need to get out of officiating. The days of your mundane G.A.A. play days are gone."

I tried to suck the words back into my mouth, realizing that I may have offended her. After all, she did have a short fuse. But I was frustrated. Fans scream and yell at boys' athletic contests all of the time. And as girls' sports programs grow, fan support will grow as well. If female athletes, coaches, and officials demand equality in sports, they had better become hardened to the accompanying pressures and heat of competition. That includes loud and sometimes fanatical fans.

With eyes blazing, the official barked at me. "Coach, I will continue to penalize your team for the derogatory comments from your fans." She subsequently turned and glared at our boys' cheerblock. Suddenly with a dramatic sweep of her arm toward the boys, she hollered, "You first three rows are outta here!"

A loud collective gasp came from our crowd and Mr. Lemna marched toward the referee. I grabbed his arm and pulled him back toward our fans. With Mr. Lemna at my side, I stood in front of our fans and raised my arms to silence the murmurs rippling through the crowd. Mr. Lemna put his index finger to his lips and exhaled a loud "Shhhh" toward the crowd.

I pleaded to our fans. "You first three rows of boys have been instructed to leave the gymnasium because of your derogatory comments toward the other team. Please, for me and the team, exit calmly. We don't want to forfeit the match!"

The boys in the first three rows stood silently and began descending from the bleachers. Mr. Lemna nodded to me and began leading them toward the exit.

As the guys proceeded to march across the floor, the Carmel High School fans erupted with clapping and cheers. In a spontaneous final act of defiance, one of our boys shouted above the roar, "Give me a 'D'." "Give me an 'E'," another hollered. "Give me an 'R'," they continued as they proudly stomped across the floor chanting and spelling the word D-E-R-O-G-A-T-O-R-Y. "What's that spell? DEROGATORY!" they yelled collectively as the exit door closed behind them.

Avoiding the referee's glare, I rushed across the court to rejoin my team, who stood like statues with bewildered expressions from witnessing the chaos. *I've got to calm them down,* I thought. I was fearful that they would be rattled from all of the commotion. My fears were real, as Carmel claimed the next five points once play resumed. Our remaining fans resumed a polite decorum as the momentum shifted to favor Carmel.

Because the end wall of the gymnasium featured a row of floor-to-ceiling length windows, the boys who had been banished from the gym stood with their faces pressed against the glass. They were jumping and clapping, even though they couldn't be heard from inside the gym. The visual of muted cheering inspired me. I called another time-out.

"Look at your fans!" I hollered to my girls as I motioned toward the windows. "Don't let them down. Don't let their ejection be in vain." I chuckled to myself as the words came from my mouth. *Did I really say that? Their ejection be in vain? How lame!*

Liz proceeded to serve an ace point. Annie fiercely spiked a ball to the ground. Carmel rallied to take a 14-12 lead, only a point away from winning the game. With our crowd cheering wildly and the boys banging on the windows, we tied at 14-14. Kasey served a ball that landed just inside Carmel's back court line. 15-14! On the subsequent play Sallie had a monstrous block on a Carmel spike. 16-14! The match was over, and we were regional champs! We were headed to the state finals for the third straight year.

The referee descended from her tower, signed the scorebook, and quickly scurried out of the gym without speaking to anyone. My body shook as I absorbed the chain of events that had just transpired. Mr. Lemna approached me and assured me that everything was okay. He was supportive of our team and fans.

"If women want to have all of the privileges of sports competition, they'd better grow thicker skins," he muttered. "If referees and female athletes can't stand the heat, then they better get out of the kitchen!"

I laughed and gave him a hug. "Thanks for your support. Apparently that official is an old fuddy-duddy from past years of 'girls should only play for fun and let's not dare hurt anyone's feelings'!" I snickered. "Not that I condone what those boys were shouting, but this is a new age for women in sports. It's a whole new environment and they'll have to learn to take the good with the not so good."

He concurred. "On to state!"

"Yep, where we may have to play against boys!" I muttered as I sprinted to join my girls in their jubilant on-court celebration.

At school on Monday morning following the regional, several members of the boys' cheerblock paraded into the gym to see me. They were all wearing identical red T-shirts with "Northside Boys' Cheerblock" printed on the front in large blue letters. Without saying a word they simultaneously turned around revealing their backs. Each guy had a different phrase printed on the back of his shirt: *Row 1 Seat 13*; *Row 2 Seat 10*; *Row 1 Seat 17*; *Row 3 Seat 15*. All around school the guys who had been ejected from the regional were proudly wearing T-shirts that identified the seat in which they had been sitting. I couldn't hold back my laughter when I saw their shirts, and thanked them for their support, but added a note of caution.

"We can't afford to lose points for unsportsmanlike conduct at state," I told them. "Please cheer enthusiastically *for* our team rather than *against* the other team." In the back of my mind, however, I anticipated that our boys' cheerblock would practice little restraint when they witnessed boys playing against their girls.

*****

South Bend Clay had indeed won their northern regional and would be joining us and six other regional winners at the state tournament. The state pairings had Northside in the opposite bracket from Clay, which meant we would meet them in the final championship match if we both won our preliminary matches. Without doubt, the history-making battle between my girls and the boys would make for a raucous final. I felt conflicted, however. Whereas I loved the enthusiasm and support of our boys' cheerblock, I was also a strong proponent of sportsmanlike behavior. I was extremely proud that my players' conduct had been exemplary. Fans were more difficult to control. Crowd control and rabidity of fans was an emerging factor in girls' sports.

As I watched the adolescent boys walk out of the gym exuberantly punching each other, I shuddered at the thought of the nasty heckling that Brian Goralski and his teammate, Ed Derse, might face once our boys saw them spiking volleyballs at our girls. *I can't worry about that, though,* I thought. *My job is to make sure my girls can dig up those bullet spikes.*

Dave Shondell and the boys' cheerblock

CHAPTER 17

CAREER DECISIONS

There are times in your life when you feel like you're on a speeding train that keeps accelerating. As it flies down the track and you look out the window, everything is a blur. Then, occasionally there is an abrupt stop, crash, or derailment. This pause often causes you to step back and re-evaluate. Amid the flurry of activity, with our wedding only five weeks away and the state tournament fast approaching, my train came to an abrupt halt a few days after regionals. I received a telephone call from a man I didn't know, but who could potentially change my life.

"Is this the Debbie Millbern who plays basketball?" he asked.

I was momentarily stunned by the question since I had told the Marion-Kay Peppers that I was not playing for them this season. "That's me," I answered.

"My name is Roger Carroll and I'm a representative of the new Women's Professional Basketball League. You have an opportunity to be drafted by one of our teams. It'll most likely be the Milwaukee Does."

"Professional basketball for women?" I stammered. "A league?"

"Absolutely. There are some investors organizing an eight-team professional league, and you are one of the players we're recruiting to play in it," Mr. Carroll stated.

I felt the blood rush from my brain and was beginning to feel light-headed. I was finding it hard to choke out my words as my mind was swirling. "Do you mean I'll get paid…to play *basketball*?"

"Yep," he answered. "If it's okay I can be in Muncie on Tuesday and I'd like to sit down with you in person to discuss it. Can you meet me in the lobby of the Holiday Inn at 5:00 p.m.?"

"That'll be great. I'll be there Mr. Carroll. Thank you!"

I hung up the phone and immediately called Jim. "You need to get over here…now! I've been offered an opportunity to play professional basketball."

I sank into the sofa in a state of shock as I waited for Jim to drive over. What was this about? Who was this Roger Carroll? Was this really going to happen? Images from my past bounced through my brain in the form of still-framed pictures…my boastful declarations to my parents that I was going to play professional basketball someday…the essay that I wrote in Mrs. Middlebury's ninth-grade English class telling her the same… my tearful prayers of yearning to play on a team…the hours spent on the driveway pretending to win NBA championships…and the final stark pain that hit me when I found our there was no such opportunity for women. Was that eleven-year-old girl's fantasy finally becoming a reality?

Once Jim arrived I told him about my brief conversation with Mr. Carroll. I paced back and forth across the living room while I talked. It was hard to control my excitement. Jim had more questions than I had answers.

"When does this start?" "How long is the season?" "How much do you get paid?" "What if you get injured?" "What would you do during the off-season?" "Where would we live?" And one more very important question: "What would *I* do in Milwaukee?" he asked.

"These are the things to discuss with Mr. Carroll when I meet with him on Tuesday," I reassured him. "Will you please go with me? I need you there so that I ask all the right questions and don't miss anything," I pleaded.

"I wouldn't miss it," Jim responded with a broad smile.

The Holiday Inn lobby was dimly lit as the Tuesday afternoon sun was setting. Entering through the revolving door I breathed in a pungent scent of cigarette smoke intermingled with a hint of vanilla air freshener. The lobby was decorated with a medieval theme. Huge iron light fixtures dangled from heavy chains throughout the room. Amber teardrop light bulbs flickered inside each fixture giving an absurd appearance of real flames. Red shag carpet and cheap leather chairs accented with decorative nail heads completed the castle-like décor.

"All we need is a moat," Jim snorted as he surveyed the unusually garish lobby.

A man rose from a round table situated near a window. He was carrying a leather brief case and extended his right hand as he walked toward me.

"You must be Debbie."

"Yes," I answered. "And this is my fiancé, Jim Powers."

"Roger Carroll," the man said as he shook Jim's hand. Mr. Carroll motioned us to his table.

Roger Carroll was average in height and build. I estimated that he was in his early fifties. His hair, or toupee, as I guessed, was a light brown that clashed with his blondish sideburns. He wore black-rimmed glasses and had a ruddy complexion. His red and gray plaid sport coat would make Coach Bob Knight envious. His handshake was firm, yet inviting.

"I'll give you the basics, Debbie, and then I'll answer your questions."

I opened a spiral notebook to take notes.

Mr. Carroll began speaking. "Several investors believe that the time is right for a professional women's basketball league. It'll be called the Women's Basketball League, or WBL for short. I am a member of a national scouting service scouring the country and identifying the best women players. We're looking at outstanding AAU players and current college players who will be graduating soon. There will hopefully be eight teams: Houston, Milwaukee, New York, Dayton, New Jersey, Chicago, Minnesota, and Iowa. Each team will play a thirty-four-game season. Your best bet is to go with the Milwaukee Does."

I quickly jotted the team locations into my notebook. "When would I report to Milwaukee?"

"The details haven't been worked out yet, but we hope to have the first game by December, 1978."

"But it's only 1975. That's three years away," I responded.

"Right, but the teams would be have to be assembled and practicing within the next year or two. There's a lot to do yet with publicity, marketing, franchising, promotions, game sites, scheduling, officials, and coaches. Plus, once people see women playing basketball in next summer's Olympics, we think the popularity and enthusiasm for the league will skyrocket."

"How long is the season? What months would we play?" I asked.

"It looks like the season would be about five months, December into May, with an all-star game and a league championship thrown in. Like I said, the details haven't been worked out yet. We need first to line up all the investors and get you players committed to training camps."

"So I would sign a contract? And how much would I be paid?"

"Absolutely, you would commit to a one-year contract, to be renewed yearly depending on your performance and other factors. The average player's salary being tossed around is $5,000."

I glanced at Jim. He hadn't said a word yet, but his posturing told me that he wasn't delighted with what he was hearing. I continued taking notes in my notebook.

"Mr. Carroll," Jim interrupted, "What will these players do for income the other seven months of the year? Do you provide them jobs?"

Mr. Carroll smiled. "It depends on their skills, talent, and education. We'll help them the best we can to find work in local offices, factories, or retail stores."

Jim and I looked at each other. I knew he was reading my mind. *What kind of job could I get for part of a year, May until December? I certainly couldn't teach!* I thought.

"This isn't exactly the NBA, is it, Mr. Carroll?" I said, unable to curtail a sarcastic tone.

"Of course not, but it's a start. We eventually hope to build a huge fan base, and gals like you can showcase your talents to the world."

I put my pencil down and leaned back in my chair. My head was swirling with a barrage of questions and scenarios, and my enthusiasm for this opportunity was fading with each answer I received.

"So, what do you think?" Mr. Carroll asked.

I closed my notebook and stood up. "I really have to think about this, Mr. Carroll. Jim and I are getting married in a few weeks, so it's not just my future that I have to consider."

Mr. Carroll stood and reached inside his briefcase. "Of course. I understand. Take my card and give me a call if you have any other questions or concerns. We'll need to know your decision by February."

We walked to the front door of the lobby and Mr. Carroll shook my hand. "I really, really hope you'll play for us," he said as he continued shaking my hand vigorously.

Jim and I rode in the car for several miles without talking. Finally he broke the silence. "Let's stop and get a bite to eat," he said.

We slid into a private booth at Denny's and ordered food before I spoke. The aroma of coffee and grilled hamburgers filled my senses, along with the clanking sound of dishes being collected by bus boys. I swirled the ice in my glass with a straw and sighed. "I'm not going to do it."

Jim looked at me with penetrating eyes. "But you......"

"No, let me talk," I interrupted. "You have no idea how many times I've dreamed of playing basketball as a profession. The hours and hours of practicing with hopes of it becoming a reality. The tears I shed when I had to sit on the sidelines as a young girl. How much I wanted to have a shiny uniform, a real coach, adoring fans. I loved playing basketball more than anything else in the world. But you know what? I'm not intoxicated with that dream anymore. I've found two new loves—*you* and *coaching*. What happens when we want to start a family? I certainly couldn't play then! No, I want to continue coaching young women to pursue *their* athletic dreams and to reach *their* goals. I want to help them grow through sports and give them the opportunities that I didn't have. Besides, this new WBL sounds pretty shaky. There's no money in it, no security, and no longevity. As much as I would love to play professional basketball, I just don't feel good about this new league."

Jim reached across the table and stroked my hand. We sat in silence for a minute.

"Don't worry. I'm not sad," I reassured him. "I'm past it. I'm moving on."

*****

In preparation for the state tournament I asked some of the male athletes from the cheerblock to come to our practices and scrimmage against my girls. It was the only way I knew to prepare the girls to face bigger blocks and harder hits. I had not seen South Bend

Clay's team play, nor did I know any coaches who had played them during the season. Scouting other teams was unheard of in girls' sports. There were no films of matches to study, or assistant coaches to send on scouting trips. Because most women coaches were overworked with a full load of teaching and the burdens of coaching multiple sports, there was no time to travel to opponents' contests. As a result, I had no idea how Clay utilized Brian's and Ed's skills, where they lined up, or if they or their team had any weaknesses. All I could do was drill my girls to adjust to any circumstances we might face. Just like all season, our first look at our opponent would be on the court.

The boys added freshness and fun to our practices. We had lively scrimmages and the girls adjusted to the offensive and defensive changes I proposed. The guys did exactly what I asked of them, playing carefully enough not to hurt the girls, but hard enough to challenge them to adjust to their height and power. Most of the guys had played intramural volleyball, so they knew the game, and were decent players. The most important factor was that they were big and strong.

Publicity about the upcoming controversial state tournament was beginning to emerge. Mr. Lemna showed me the newest *Sports Illustrated* which had a paragraph in their "Scorecard" section commenting about Brian Goralski playing on the girls' volleyball team in South Bend, Indiana. The article talked about tiny all-girl St. Mary's Academy losing to South Bend Clay in their sectional. Afterward, the St. Mary's principal and athletic director petitioned the IHSAA to issue a directive eliminating boys from playing in the remaining volleyball championship series on the grounds that Title IX, being federal legislation, supersedes and invalidates the IHSAA rule allowing boys to compete on girls' teams. Their petition argued that the under Title IX guidelines it is not necessary that there be comparable *programs* for males and females, but merely comparable *opportunities* to participate in a fall sport. In response to the petition, IHSAA commissioner Phil Eskew refused to budge, stating: "So sue me."

Mr. Lemna also told me that an article went out on the national Associated Press circuit. Knowing that Northside was the defending state champion and favored to meet Clay in the finals, friends and colleagues of Mr. Lemna's had been calling him and reading headlines from their local sports sections:

Bend, OR: **"Indiana Boy Harassed for
               Competing with Girls"**
Gettysburg, PA: **"Girls Court Case to Get on Golf
               Team Leads to Boy on Volleyball Team"**
Fredericksburg, VA: **"Goralski Making Point on
               Girls' Team"**
Paris, TX: **"Girls' Volleyball Tough for Boy"**

Brian Goralski had a quote in these articles: *"The people I go to school with are all for me. They want the team to win the state tournament,"* he stated.

Clay's coach, Joan Mitchell, was also quoted: *"I don't think it's fair for the boys to play against the girls, but I understand his purpose in coming out for the team---to try to bring attention to the fact that boys need a boys' volleyball team. And, I just can't see any way that I can say that they can't play if they make my team."*

My hope was that these headlines and quotes motivated my girls as much as I felt the drive to compete.

I heard that a contingent of female coaches was planning to travel to Indianapolis to protest to the IHSAA within the next few days. One of the coaches called me, begging me to accompany them.

"We cannot tolerate this," she told me on the phone. "We've come too far to allow boys to dominate our sport."

I agreed and sympathized with her. "But at this late date I doubt if anything can be done."

"Come with us, Debbie. Your presence would mean a lot."

Even though I felt strongly against the boys, I was a realist. Both the courts and the IHSAA had spoken. The state final was only days away. I also realized that my team had the most at stake if we made it to the final game. After all, we were the defending state champions who could lose to *boys* in a girls' state championship!

"Even though I sympathize with the cause, I can't afford to take the time or be distracted from my job this week of preparing my team physically and mentally to beat those guys. Beating them on the volleyball court rather than in the court room will be *my* statement. Then we'll have to work to prevent this from happening in future years." I hung up the phone feeling slightly like a traitor to these women, but I had to keep focused on my immediate task.

"Do you think you can beat them?" Jim asked me.

"I don't know, but we're going to try our darnedest."
Jim smiled. "If anyone can, it'll be you."

It was comforting to have Jim around to share my
anxieties as well as my joys during this stressful time.
With our wedding only five weeks away and the added
flurry of activity as I prepared for the state finals, my
decision regarding the professional basketball
opportunity evaporated from my consciousness. I was
absorbed into a new challenging endeavor that filled my
competitive tank.

The atmosphere at school was amazing. The
hallways of Northside High School overflowed with
excitement the week before the state finals. Colorful
hand-painted signs designed by the art classes covered
the painted walls and hung from the ceilings:

**"Northside fans say set 'em high and spike 'em
low. Come on girls, let's go!"**

"Win State...Again!"

"Bring home the bacon, Titans!"

"Millbern's got the POWER(s)"

An all-school pep rally was being planned for
Friday. Good luck cards and notes were filling my
mailbox. Mr. Carmichael even reserved several rooms
at an Indianapolis hotel for the team to rest between the
Saturday morning and evening sessions. The *Muncie
Star* published articles. Reporters from the
Indianapolis Star and *Louisville Courier-Journal* called
to interview me. Excitement was building. Thankfully

my team continued to work hard in practice without letting the hype and publicity about the boys on Clay's team affect them. They acted like they knew what they were facing. My question was…did they really?

"Look how well we play against Wes, Steve, Dave, and all those guys in practice," Kasey stated as she bounced a volleyball repeatedly against the floor during a post-practice huddle.

"Those Clay guys don't have a chance," Annie added while playfully swatting at Kasey's ball.

Sallie flexed her muscles as if in a body-builder's pose. "They don't know who they're messin' with."

I loved hearing their comments, and I vocally affirmed every one of them with passion. Having eight seniors who had played in the previous three state tournaments would be a boost for us. They oozed confidence and leadership.

"We will continue to work hard in our preparation," I said to the team. "And, we will not make excuses---win or lose."

On Thursday evening, two days before we were to travel to the state tournament, Jim and I were relaxing in my apartment. We ordered a Pizza King royal feast pizza and shared a bottle of wine.

"Remember our first shared Pizza King pizza?" I asked as I let a bite of the juicy delight slide down my throat.

"Sure do," Jim responded. "Just about a year ago."

I was perusing the *Indianapolis Star* sports section while we were eating. "Hey, listen to this: **'Titan Girls Lead Volleyball Field'**." I read the headline aloud using a booming sports reporter voice. *"Muncie appears to be the team to beat because it has most of its* *championship team back. South Bend Clay, with two boys on the team, could emerge as the top threat to Muncie's title."*

I laid the paper down and leaned back in my chair. "Do you suppose we will be reading about this same kind of thing happening twenty years from now?"

Jim took a sip of wine. "What kind of thing?"

"Boys being allowed to play on girls' teams, of course!"

"Who knows? It seems pretty ridiculous to me because the guys would eventually dominate," Jim responded.

I banged my hand on the table. "Of course they would! Hopefully by then people will accept separate but equal sports opportunities, and appreciate *all* athletes' abilities, regardless of gender."

Suddenly the telephone rang, interrupting our conversation. I dashed across the room and picked up the receiver. "Hello. This is Debbie."

"Debbie, this is Eileen Keener, the women's athletic director at Ball State University. I'm calling to inform you that our head women's basketball coach has announced that she'll be leaving at the end of the season. I would like for you to strongly consider interviewing for the open position."

I looked over at Jim, who was happily munching on another wedge of pizza and reading more of the paper. The first thought that popped into my head was that this was a voice from God. *Ball State University...less than a mile from my apartment and an NCAA Division I program. Basketball...my preferred sport. Head coach...at age 25.*

I felt my breathing accelerate and choked out a response. "Thank you, Mrs. Keener, for considering me."

"Well, Debbie," she continued, "I watched you play against us during the years you were at Indiana University. You were such a fine player. And now you have proven yourself as a talented young coach at Northside. You were the first person we thought of to lead our growing program. And I think you'll be excited to know that we'll soon be offering athletic scholarships to women."

My hand holding the receiver was quivering, so I pressed the receiver hard to my ear to steady my hand.

"If I'm selected for this position, when would I start?" I asked. I glanced at Jim who was still reading the paper. Overhearing my question, he abruptly set down his wine glass and stared at me.

"Oh, it wouldn't be until next August, at the start of school year. And, it is a tenure-line, full-benefits position with part-time teaching responsibilities in our school of physical education."

"Mrs. Keener, I have to say I am *very* interested."

"Terrific! The committee will be delighted to hear that. I know you have a big weekend ahead of you, so I'll call you within the next few weeks to set up an interview."

"Thank you so much for the opportunity, Mrs. Keener," I replied.

"Good luck at the state tournament." She paused, and then spoke with a tone of disgust, "What a travesty."

"I know. Good-bye and thanks again."

I put the phone down and grinned at Jim. I began jumping up and down.

"What?" he asked. His bewildered look amused me.

"I may have resolved our problem of what to do next year when one of us is forced to leave Northside."

CHAPTER 18

ON OUR WAY

The atmosphere at the state finals could be described in one word---wild. Because eight teams would be battling for the right to play in the evening final match, the arena was tightly packed with fans from every school during the morning sessions. The monochrome bleachers became a patchwork of school colors. Families and fans proudly donned the golds, blues, grays, reds, purples, and greens that identified their allegiances. When two schools were playing a match, their fans would be chanting and cheering while the remaining unaffected crowd politely applauded good plays. There was a noticeably large contingency of feminists who held signs announcing their disdain for South Bend Clay:

"GO HOME BRIAN AND ED!"
"NO BOYS ALLOWED!"
"JOAN MITCHELL IS A TRAITOR."
"HEY GIRLS...BEAT THE BOYS!"

These bold, hand-written words established a tone of scattered discontent throughout the arena.

I was pleased to play our preliminary matches before Clay would take the floor. That fit perfectly with my scheme of not allowing my girls to see Clay's team play until we faced them at the night's final match. I could send them off with their parents to get away from the arena while I stayed to watch the other matches.

It took awhile to shake our nerves in our first match against Wayne High School of Fort Wayne. Even my seniors seemed stiff and tentative. I was even more surprised at how nervous I was. My gut felt like a volcano was erupting inside. Because we were defending champions, a majority of the crowd rooted for Wayne throughout our match. We weren't used to such a huge number of people cheering against us, and we lost the first game, 11-15.

"Everyone loves an upset," I hollered at my team during a timeout. "Let's not satisfy their wishes. Let's disappoint them!"

Thankfully the team responded, and we bounced back to win the next two games, 15-5, 15-7. Our boys' cheerblock was rambunctious and loud throughout the match, but surprisingly polite toward our opponents.

Our second match was easier. The girls played with the confidence and fervor that was our trademark. We downed Castle High School in two quick games. We were now headed to the final championship match.

"We're only one match short of our goal!" I yelled to the girls as they jogged off the court toward our bench and me. I was impressed with their businesslike approach. Like me, they were not celebrating yet. In fact, I could practically read the words "unfinished business" on each of their faces.

After the match the Northside parents gathered their daughters and took them to the hotel to rest before the evening session. Jim and I stayed at the arena. I was anxious to watch South Bend Clay and especially Brian Goralski play volleyball. We climbed to an isolated spot high up in the arena away from rowdy spectators where I could concentrate on the match.

The atmosphere in the arena changed dramatically when the South Bend Clay players ran onto the floor. The air was filled with boos and hisses toward the Clay team. My initial reaction was to feel sorry for the eight girls on the Clay team. This couldn't be a positive sports experience for them to constantly hear the taunts that weren't personally directed at them. The crowd's disdain was naturally directed toward Brian Goralski, Ed Derse, and their coach, Joan Mitchell.

Brian was lean and muscular. He towered above the girls. As I watched him warm up I realized that none of the boys against whom we had practiced during the week came close to his superior abilities. The entire arena gasped when he leaped high into the air to spike the ball. His head and powerful arms were high above the net, and the ball resounded against the floor like a cannon blast. My first question was how to block him. It would be impossible since most of my players are lucky to get their forearms above the net. He'd be hitting the ball far above their outstretched fingers. His serve was even scarier. He jumped in the air and hit a powerful roundhouse serve that blasted across the net with heavy topspin. In Clay's first game his serve knocked down two opposing girls as if they were bowling pins. His spikes were so powerful that the opponents began cowering rather than attempting to dig them up. I looked at Jim with panic in my eyes. "Holy crap! We're in trouble," I muttered. Ed was not as talented as Brian, but he was another strong force at the net, being 6'0" tall. I jotted a few notes in my notebook pertaining to Clay's alignments and prayed silently for a miracle.

After watching Clay annihilate the other teams, Jim drove me to the hotel to meet with my team. They were all assembled in one room eating pizza and watching television. I stepped over empty pizza boxes as I entered the room. Once they saw me, the girls plopped onto the beds and sat cross-legged, staring at me with wide-eyed anticipation.

"Well, how good is he?" Kasey asked.

"Did Clay win?" Shelley added.

"Whaddya think, Coach?" Annie chimed in.

If an Academy Award for acting were to be given at that moment, I would have rightfully received it. I casually leaned against the door frame and crossed my arms in front of my chest. "Girls," I said with the broadest smile I could muster, "we can win this! He's not nearly as good as the boys we've practiced against all week."

The girls began screaming and jumping on the bed. The slapping sound of high fives filled the room.

"Get your bags together and be on the bus in fifteen minutes," I hollered above the melee. *What a liar I am,* I thought as I exited the room.

With the team already on the bus, George sat in the driver's seat adjusting the defroster. Thin sheets of ice slid down the windshield like tiny floating islands. As

I waited on the sidewalk and shuffled my feet to keep warm, I saw Susie emerge from the hotel lobby struggling to carry a cumbersome mesh bag of volleyballs, a canvas tote of towels, and the steel-case athletic training kit.

"Here, Susie, let me give you a hand," I said, as I swung my purse over my shoulder and hurried toward her to grab the bag of balls.

"Thanks, Coach Millbern. I'm pretty sure I have everything we need."

I smiled and winked at her. "I hope you packed a little bit of luck in there too."

She grinned. "Don't worry. They're ready, Coach. You've prepared them well."

"You're always the optimist, Susie. Thank you."

Susie nodded and climbed the bus steps. I heard whooping and clapping coming from the bus as the team acknowledged Susie's arrival. I followed Susie into the bus and, like her, was greeted by the clapping and chanting team.

"Okay. Okay." I smiled and waved to them. I stood at the front of the bus, hanging onto the overhead silver rail with both hands. Everyone became silent and all their eyes were on me. "Let's save some of that energy for the match!" I shouted. After a collective, loud "Yeahhh!" from the group, they quieted down again.

"Right now I want all of you to check your bags. Look to see that you have your full uniform and your shoes." All heads disappeared below the seats and I heard multiple bags zipping open. Sometimes I felt like their mother, barking reminders and warnings, even though I was only a few years older than the seniors on the team.

"Tonight is not the night to show up without any part your uniform," I told them. "And you know I speak from experience." They all laughed and waved to Holly. Holly, one of our new players this year, had forgotten to pack her shoes for one match during the season and, as a result, had to sit and watch from the bleachers. It was a painful lesson for everyone, and especially embarrassing for her, since her grandparents had traveled 125 miles to watch her play.

"Everyone have their player pass for admission back into the arena?" I asked. I saw multiple hands lift and wave small laminated cards in the air.

"Saaaaayyyyyy, aren't we *big-time* having State Championship passes?" I yelled as I waved my pass in the air. Another round of loud whooping and hollering erupted.

"Everyone's family coming tonight?" I asked.

Several "yes's" filled the air, along with shouts of "my grandma and grandpa," "my aunt," "my brother," "my neighbors." Everyone quieted again and only the soft rumble of the bus engine could be heard underfoot.

"Hey, Coach," Liz yelled to me. "Are your parents here?" Momentary sadness hit me, and I struggled to hide the tone of disappointment in my voice.

"No, they couldn't come. They live in Florida, too far away."

Of course I had invited my parents to the state finals. They were the first people I had called when we won the regional championship to qualify for state. I was so excited and sure that they would want to come. They had never seen me coach, and this was a huge event. I told them how monumental it was to be playing against boys and how there had been a lot of publicity surrounding these finals. But they didn't seem very interested. It hurt a lot, and I was especially surprised by my dad's indifference. My guess was that Mom made the decision that they would not make the long and expensive trip to Indiana.

I quickly switched my thoughts back to the present. "But," I said to the team, "my fiancé will be there." From my bag I pulled two red roses that had been delivered to me earlier in the day and waved them in the air.

"Hear, hear for Mr. Powers!" a voice shouted from the back of the bus. The rest of the team whistled and clapped.

I turned to George. "Let's get going," I said.

George pulled on the huge lever to close the bus door and pressed the gear shift into first. We were on our way.

As the bus headed down the highway, I looked out the window at the passing corn fields. Even though the daylight was fading into darkness, many farmers were still working in their fields. With penetrating headlights, huge combines moved slowly along the perfectly formed rows as tall tubes sprayed corn into large trucks. The vehicles looked like huge science-fiction creatures. Seeing the harvest was just one of the things I loved about fall in Indiana. Another delight was watching the trees become a kaleidoscope of color against a backdrop of blue sky. Individual leaves fell like snow flakes, slowly twirling their way to the ground. Dried leaves crackled underfoot, and, after a rain, the smell of damp leaves filled the air. Fall in Indiana was a smorgasbord for the senses.

For me though, the best part of fall had always been the commencing of basketball season. Within a month all the gymnasiums in Indiana would be filled with the sounds of bouncing balls, blowing whistles, and rubber-soled shoes squeaking on the hardwood. Even though I was currently immersed in coaching volleyball, my innermost soul still quivered with excitement in anticipation of basketball season. I still felt a wisp of anxiety having turned down the professional playing opportunity. But coaching basketball at Ball State would be a dream, even though it would be hard to say good-bye to these high school girls I'd come to adore.

My mind drifted to last year's trip to the state volleyball finals. It seemed so long ago now, yet it was still mind-boggling what that team had accomplished with its perfect record and state championship under the guidance of such a novice coach. That thrill of winning never escapes you, and you want to experience that feeling again and again. Of course this season had a re-configured team and a new set of circumstances. With the challenges and distraction this team had faced, I felt like a character in an exciting sports movie. I could visualize a dramatic big-screen montage showing bits and pieces of this season finally coming together, accompanied by a feel-good soundtrack marking the high point that brings tears to the viewers' eyes. Regardless of the final outcome, people always love it when problems are resolved or challenges are met. This 1975 team had come together and faced its biggest challenge tonight.

The bus rumbled to a stop, jolting me from my reverie. The girls had been singing along to the tunes on the bus radio.

"Taking care of business, everyday. Taking care of business everyway......."

"That's the way, uh huh, uh huh, I like it, uh huh, uh huh......"

I chuckled to myself. *I sure hope they're ready to take care of business tonight on the court. Because if they do, they'll like it for the rest of their lives!*

The arena parking lot was filling quickly and a policeman directed our bus to a spot close to the building. As soon as the bus stopped, I grabbed the bag of balls and was the first one off the bus.

"Go get 'em, Coach," I heard George, our driver, shout behind me. I nodded back to him.

After the girls were off the bus, we all stood quietly together looking up at the giant arena. Finally, Kasey broke the silence. "No different than our gym. We proved that this morning," she said with an air of confidence. Several of the girls giggled and murmured in agreement as we began walking toward the illuminated entrance.

A middle-aged, balding man met us at the door. He wore gray pants and a matching gray shirt. He had a ring of at least twenty keys attached to his belt that jingled with every step he took. He shook my hand and introduced himself as Harold, and told us that he would show us to our locker room. Spectators were milling around the concession stands as we headed down the wide corridor. Several appeared to be female volleyball coaches chaperoning their young athletes. Many wore their team jerseys. Juggling popcorn boxes and Cokes, several fans clapped and shouted encouragement to us when they saw us.

"Good luck, Northside."

"Don't back down, girls."

"Beat their sorry asses, Northside."

"We're behind you, Coach Millbern."

"Show 'em what girls can do."

I saw several of my team nod their heads, acknowledging their comments. I smiled and motioned a "thumbs up" to the other coaches.

We passed one of the large double doors that opened onto the arena floor. I peeked in and saw the head referees in their striped shirts measuring and adjusting the net. The scorekeepers were busy assembling their materials. The timekeeper was fiddling with some long cords. Illuminated by huge overhead lights, the court floor was bright and shiny. A gray-haired female usher standing near the door saw me and rushed over to hand me a program.

"Here ya go, Coach. Hope ya kill 'em."

The program had a picture of my team on the front cover from last year's championship. Sticking out of the program was a loose sheet of paper with a purple mimeographed paragraph typed on it. I pulled it out and read the heading as I continued walking down the hall: *An Open Letter to Coach Joan Mitchell … …* I read the first few lines.

You are a disgrace to girls' sports. You are a traitor. If you really had courage, you'd put six GIRLS on the floor to be worthy of winning the GIRLS' state championship. Congratulations … … you have set girls' sports back ten years in Indiana.

I stopped reading, folded the paper, and slipped it into my bag. I didn't want to read any further. I had expected that a group of women coaches would probably protest in some way at the final match. My focus at this moment had to be on more important things like preparing my team. I didn't need distractions or negativity.

Harold unlocked the heavy steel door to our locker room. The words "MEN VISITORS" were stenciled on the door. *How funny*, I thought. *I wonder if South Bend Clay has the word "men" stenciled on their locker room door.* We entered the locker room to the combined smell of sweat and English Leather. The girls scattered to choose their lockers as I thanked Harold for his assistance.

He responded, "You just let me know if there is anything you need this evening. Here's the key. Just be sure to lock up the room when you come to the court, and hang onto the key. I'll collect it after the match."

He handed me a single key attached by a short chain to a six-inch wooden dowel that looked like it had been part of a broom handle. As I turned away from Harold, he hesitated and reached out to touch my arm.

"I hope you beat the pants off them tonight, Coach," he said. He continued, "I have daughters, you know."

I smiled at him and walked back into the locker room and handed the key to Susie, our manager. Since my nerves were starting to tingle and my stomach churn, I couldn't trust myself to keep track of the key. I could count on Susie.

As the girls chatted and began changing into their uniforms, I walked to the far end of the locker room and sat down on one of the benches. I eyed a jock strap lying under the bench and kicked it toward the trash can. I looked around at the gray lockers, gray benches, gray concrete floors, gray walls, and gray trash can. I concluded that women had not been consulted in the decorating of locker rooms. We were definitely in a man's world, urinals and all.

I closed my eyes and began trying to formulate the final, motivating words that I would use to inspire my team. Phrases like "Win one for the Gipper" and "There's no 'I' in TEAM" seemed trite and meaningless. No girls' team had faced what we were about to face for a state championship. It was new territory. What could I say to inspire them?

The petitions, protests, newspaper articles, and meetings over the past week stating the injustices about tonight's match were yesterday's news. The attempts to stop it had failed. I had told the team during this week's practice sessions that many situations in life are not fair. Tonight's final match was one of those unjust situations, but it was reality. It was going to happen--- my team of girls was going to play for the 1975 Indiana Girls' State Volleyball Championship against a team with boys on it. It was still inconceivable to me how this could have been allowed to happen. But we'd have to deal with it---big, strong boys spiking balls across the net at my girls. I reminded myself that Kathrine Switzer had faced up to the male establishment in the 1967 Boston Marathon, and Billie Jean King had taken care of Bobby Riggs in the Battle of the Sexes. I had even whipped a few boys in my past! I wanted to win *our* battle so badly that I ached from the top of my head to the tip of my toes. I desperately wanted to beat those boys and that coach. As a player, I would have been all charged up and ready to compete. But I was now a *coach*. How much impact could I have on the outcome?

I looked at the girls who were now all nervously sitting on the locker room benches waiting for my final instructions. Some were silently looking down at the floor. Some were double-tying their shoestrings. Others were fidgeting with their hair ribbons. Oh, how I hoped that each player had my same competitive fire roaring in her core.

"Gather around everybody," I told the team. "We'll be taking the floor in a few minutes and I have something to say."

The girls scooted close together on the benches. Some draped their arms over their teammates' shoulders. All of their eager eyes were glued to me. I cleared my throat and began my speech.

"Tonight's the night we've been preparing for since the first day of practice. When we started working together in August, none of us knew that we would be facing a team with boys on it tonight. And when we beat this team tonight, we will not only be state champions, but we will be making history."

I paused for a moment to collect my thoughts. I was beginning to feel the emotion of the moment. I looked from player to player, absorbing the collective intensity in their faces.

"You will not be playing tonight for just yourselves. You will be playing for all the girls sitting out there in the bleachers who *wish* they were in your shoes. But most important, you will be playing for all of your moms, aunts, older sisters, grandmothers, and great-grandmothers who never got the opportunity to play on a team, wear a uniform, or play in a sport representing their schools. You will be playing for all those women in the past who dreamed of being an athlete, but never got the chance to be one. *You* have the opportunities that they never had. And tonight, you have the opportunity to earn a distinction few ever receive---the title *State Champion*. I am extremely honored to be your coach, and I resent that these boys have invaded *our* newfound territory. In years to come you will look back on this final match with fond memories, because it is a night that you will remember winning a state championship against incredible odds. *I* used to compete against boys all the time when I was growing up and I beat them most of the time. Now it's your turn." I hesitated and changed my calm tone to a yell. "LET'S GO BEAT ON THOSE BOYS!"

The girls grabbed each other's hands and began stomping their feet. Liz stood and began banging on a locker in a rhythmic beat. Sallie joined her. The sound reverberated throughout the locker room. After a minute of noise-making, they all stood and huddled into a tight circle with one arm in the middle of the circle, hands stacked on top of another. I wrapped my arms around as many of them as I could reach.

With their loudest voices they screamed, "BEAT THE BOYS," while raising their arms to break the circle. Tightly packed together, they jumped up in down in unison as Susie ran over and threw open the locker room door.

"Hey, wait!" Kasey yelled to everyone as she extended her arms to hold the team back from bursting through the door. "What about your poem? You *did* write a poem, didn't you, Coach?" The room suddenly got quiet and the team looked at me with expressions of anticipation.

Last season I had written a poem and read it aloud in the locker room before the state championship game. Keats, I was not, but I had written a brief rhyming jingle that the girls seemed to enjoy. Before I had gone to bed last night I scribbled another poem, and had it carefully secured in my jacket pocket. But at this moment I had decided to skip reading it because I felt the team was emotionally at a high after my brief speech. I wanted to sustain that exuberance into our warm-up out on the floor.

"Of course I wrote a poem," I said as I pulled the folded paper from my pocket. The girls retreated to their benches and got quiet. I cleared my throat and began reading......

The date today is the 15th of November,
 It will be a day in your life you will always remember.
Yes, Titans, you became one of the final eight,
 And now have a chance to win another State.
You have more experience than any team here,
 So as far as I can see, you have nothing to fear.
You have tons of ability, skill, and poise,
 And you've scrimmaged this week against the boys.
But Brian and company are waiting through that door,
 They are confident that against them you'll rarely score.
Regardless of the outcome, I know you'll play your best,
 And I love you like daughters, I surely can attest.
So to you eight seniors who to me are so dear,
 Tonight is the last time that you will ever hear......
Millbern, Millbern, open the door,
 Let those Titans on the floor!

I hadn't dared to raise my eyes from my paper while I read. The paper quivered in my hand as my emotions took hold. But I now looked up and saw my team with heads hanging low and tears flowing freely down their cheeks. It was deathly quiet. They stood slowly and began trudging silently toward the opened door, wiping their tears with their red and blue striped towels. Mel came over and gave me a hug, followed by Jill.

My heart skipped a beat. *Oh, no!* I thought. *What have I done? I had them primed and ready, and then sucked the air out of them with my sentimental poem! Dear God, I hope I haven't blown it.*

We exited the locker room and broke into an easy jog down the corridor toward the arena floor. As we got closer, the familiar chant resonated loudly from the arena.

"MILLBERN, MILLBERN OPEN THE DOOR. LET THOSE TITANS ON THE FLOOR!"

With each round of the chant, it got louder. Our boys' cheerblock was assembled and ready to rock, and I felt chills up and down my spine.

CHAPTER 19

✦

FACING THE BOYS

My team ran onto the court to a packed arena. They were greeted by raucous cheers that rebounded off every brick in the building. The noise was deafening. Since South Bend Clay had not yet emerged from their locker room, my girls jogged a full lap of the court before beginning their ball-handling drills. Several of the girls were still sniffling and wiping tears from their faces as they began setting the balls back and forth to each other. I walked toward our bench and noticed Jim sitting next to Dallas Kunkle, directly behind our bench. Jim made eye contact with me and I could easily read his mind by observing his stunned expression. It was obvious he had noticed the tears and somber looks on the faces of my girls as they jogged onto the floor, but it was so loud that all I could do was read his lips.

"What have you done?" he mouthed to me.

I shrugged my shoulders and shook my head as a silent response just as Clay ran onto the court. The cheers from the Clay fans were quickly swallowed by the loudest booing and jeering I had ever heard. The crowd unleashed itself in a passionate fury. People were standing and yelling with their hands cupped at the sides of their mouths. Obscenities were shouted directly at Clay's male players, Brian Goralski and Ed Derse. Some were mocking Brian and Ed with scathing comments:

"You guys need to shave your legs!"
"Do you wear a bra under that blouse?"
"How's it feel to beat up on girls?"

Except for the Clay fans, a majority of the spectators were not holding back voicing their disapproval of the guys playing on what should have been an all-girl team.

Our boys' cheerblock was as loud as they'd ever been---their deep voices booming out rhythmic chants. The feminists, the teams previously beaten by Clay, and every female volleyball player and coach in attendance were fiery mad. Fresh from the fervor of Billie Jean King beating Bobby Riggs, these sports-minded women were going for the jugular in these guys who were challenging my girls. The atmosphere was surreal with the chants and cheers for us intermingled with the bellowing chastisements of Clay. I realized that this was going to be much more than an athletic contest. It was going to be a war.

The six female officials, smartly dressed in their striped shirts and crisp black skirts, marched in formation onto the court. As soon as I saw them, I could not hold back a loud gasp. The woman referee who had penalized us so indiscriminately at the Carmel regional was in the group of officials! My panic subsided when I saw her take a position as one of the four line judges---an inconsequential job that solely involves calling balls in or out of the court. That role would minimize her impact on the outcome of the match, unless some latent prejudice might influence her in making a close line call. Hopefully there won't be that many balls landing so close to the lines that her temptation is fueled. I was also startled to see that another line judge, Alice Barnes, was my former teammate at Indiana University who had made a romantic gesture toward me in the locker room five years ago. Alice nodded stoically to me as she took her place on the court sideline. I was unfamiliar with the two ladies who were the designated head referees assigned to call the match. I just hoped they had thick skins.

I had never met Clay's coach, Joan Mitchell, but I greeted her politely at the scorer's table as we simultaneously turned in our starting line-ups. I saw no need for idle chat, so a brief "good luck" were our only exchanged words. She was a tall, heavy-set woman I guessed to be in her late thirties. Like me, she had her game face on, but I wondered how she'd deal with the massive derision she and her team would experience tonight.

I was glad that my players were focusing on their own warm-up routine without paying attention to Clay's pregame drills. Brian was practicing his hard-driven spikes from all over the court to the "oohs" and "aahhs" of the spectators. He was a handsome kid with a smooth baby-face and disheveled brown hair. When he walked past me toward his bench he appeared even taller than 6'3", most likely because every player around him except for his teammate, Ed, was decisively shorter. Like his coach, he had his game face on, and he ignored me. I wondered how he could enjoy playing in such a hostile environment. Was he having fun playing the sport he proclaimed to love? Or was he feeling tortured? His expression showed no emotion. As I was standing near our bench, I heard Dallas Kunkle's voice taunting Brian. "Hey Brian, you sure don't fill out your jersey like the other girls!" Dallas bellowed, followed by abundant guffawing. I felt a momentary twinge of sympathy for the poor kid.

Brian Goralski

When the buzzer sounded to end the warm-up period, the girls ran to gather around me for our final huddle. Their faces glistened with perspiration as they stared intensely at me.

I pulled them in close. "Alright. Let's stick with our strategy that we've practiced all week. Ignore the crowd and concentrate on this first game." I paused and then smiled broadly at them. "And don't forget to have fun!"

We broke from the huddle and they ran to their positions on the court. I gave a quick nod and smile to Jim as I sat down on the bench. My heart was racing. I'd experienced butterflies before, but nothing like this. I felt like there was a vise tightening on all of my internal organs.

In volleyball there are six players on the court--- three in the front row and three in the back. Only the front-row players are allowed to jump and spike the ball across the net or to block opposing spikes at the net. Back row players can spike only if they jump from behind the attack line, ten feet from the net. Few girls are tall enough or jump high enough to spike from behind this line. Brian, however, was so tall and hung so high in the air above the net, Clay could set him the ball all over the court to spike. After watching him play in the morning matches, I knew we were not simply playing South Bend Clay; it was Muncie Northside versus Brian Goralski! Rather than establish a multiple-player block, our strategy would be to send one front-row girl to attempt to block him (actually "merely get into his face," I explained to the girls). The rest of the team was to scatter to defensive positions around the court and prepare to dig up his powerful hits. On offense we would try to hit around him or lob it over him when he was at the net. When he rotated to the back row we could spike hard against the shorter girls.

"You have to know where Brian is at all times!" I had commanded my team.

Ed was not as athletic as Brian, so we'd play him as if he was a big girl, even though he still had four inches on my tallest player.

The match was to be best out of three games. The first team to score fifteen points (and be ahead by two points) wins each game. And, a team can score points only when they have the serve, which they earn by continuing to score. A game clock runs whenever the ball is in play, so a game could end if eight minutes of running time expires and one team is merely ahead by two points.

As expected Clay started Brian in the front row so he could be spiking at the net for three full rotations before moving to the back row. We chose to serve first, having won the coin toss.

It was obvious after the initial serve this match was going to be a fierce battle. Brian blasted his first powerful spike across the net, and it was dug up by Liz in a spectacular dive in the backcourt. Annie pounded the ball across the net to their floor for the first point of the match. The crowd roared and our boys' cheerblock erupted into a wild whooping frenzy with clenched fists pumping into the air. Beaming from ear to ear, Liz picked herself up from the floor and the team screamed collectively with delight. I jumped what seemed like three feet into the air off the bench.

"That's the way, Northside!" I shouted and clapped. I knew that first play would be a huge confidence-builder.

Points went back and forth with long rallies and a periodic hard hit by Brian that had my girls diving to play it up or sprawled watching the ball smack the floor out of their reach. With the score tied at 6-6, Brian rotated to the back row and served his crushing roundhouse serve. Unaffected by its speed and vicious spin, Sallie played the ball up like a professional, and Kasey slammed a hit to Clay's floor. I thought the spectators were going to lift the roof off the building with their thundering explosion of approval. Breaking Brian's initial serve was another confidence-builder for us.

Brian Goralski's powerful spike

Because the noise was so deafening, I continued to encourage my team with clapping, "thumbs-up" signals, nodding, smiling, and standing with dramatic fist-pumping. There was no way they would be able to hear my verbal instructions amid the tumultuous din. I was glad we had practiced our strategies all week, because the team was executing them to perfection without my constant hounding. I could feel the perspiration dripping down my back as I found myself in a zombie-like trance in this unrelenting competition. Like a hawk hunting for prey, I was sharply focused on every movement on the court and nothing else.

With the score tied at six, a dramatic turn of events occurred. Mel, my petite 5'5" sophomore, rotated to our back row to serve. She reeled off eight straight points, including three ace serves that no Clay player could even get a hand on. As Mel continued to serve, Brian was stuck in the back row, unable to rotate to the front row to spike or block at the net. Even though his teammates still set him to spike from the back row, he wasn't as effective because the angle and velocity of his hits were reduced. We were able to easily play them up and subsequently attack at the net. We led 14-6. The boys' cheerblock stood and stomped on the bleachers during the final rally as Sallie blocked a Clay girl's spike back into her face for the final point. We had won the first game, 15-6. My girls leaped into the air and hugged each other before sprinting over to our bench. As they sat on the bench guzzling water and wiping their sweaty faces, I could see the resolve in their eyes.

I knelt down in front of them. "Stay focused and let's do it to 'em again," I shouted. "This is *our* night, not Brian's."

The second game became an endurance contest. We jumped to a 2-0 lead, but Clay surged back to take a 10-3 lead. Brian's performance was brilliant as his spikes, blocks, and serves had my girls scrambling around the court like ants frantically working on an ant hill. After using a time-out to calm my team, they responded by scoring four straight points to close the gap to 10-7. The rallies became longer as both teams scraped and clawed for every point. Brian's sheer physical presence overtook us again as he scored four straight kills. The score was 14-7. Clay needed only one point to win the game, but the time clock was running down. With only forty seconds left, we caught fire again and were able to score three more points. The buzzer sounded. Time had run out. We had lost the second game, 14-10.

As the team gathered around me before the final, deciding game I took the time to look at each player squarely in her eyes. I could not show anger, because I was not angry at them. In fact, I felt love for them. I loved their courage and perseverance. I loved the way they were working together and supporting each other. I loved their focus in such an intense environment. They were all playing their hardest and performing at the maximum of their abilities. They were playing unbelievable volleyball against incredible odds. I realized that a few lucky breaks here and there would most likely determine the outcome of this final game. I wanted them to feel confident that they could continue playing at the same high level and win this next game.

"Well, I guess we had to let them have a game, huh?" I said with a broad smile. I could sense their relief as the tension in their faces evaporated. A few of the girls giggled.

"Come on you guys, we can do this!" Kasey shouted in the huddle.

"Yeah, this next game is ours!" Annie added.

Heads began nodding and I extended my arms to touch as many players as I could reach. "Listen to me," I spoke with a calmness that surprised me. Oblivious to

282

the perspiration dripping from their chins, their eyes pierced mine with laser-like intensity. I continued, looking from player to player, "I can tell Brian is getting tired. Let's not even try to block him at the net anymore. When they set him, I want all six of you to back off the net, get low, and be ready to dig up everything." I grabbed my program and quickly diagrammed the new defensive formation on the back cover. "Make them work hard for every ball," I shouted above the increasing decibels of noise in the arena.

Brian leaps high above the net to block.

As the girls jogged back onto the court, I entertained myself with an amusing thought: *Coaching is nothing more than an advanced form of cheerleading!* I grabbed a towel to wipe the sweat from my face and sat down on the bench. *And I always told everyone that I hated cheerleading!* I snickered to myself as I handed Susie my towel.

We started the deciding game in an improbable flurry, scoring seven unanswered points. Whether it was a temporary letdown on our part or Clay's "never give up" attitude, the rallies got longer and Clay tied us at 7-7 with Brian unleashing his power at the net. I called a time-out and substituted Jill in to serve. She was our most lethal server, and a senior. She responded by serving a rocket that passed inches above the net and landed in the back corner of Clay's court without a single player touching it. Her ace serve ignited us into another string of nail-biting rallies back and forth with Clay. I lost all sense of time and place as I watched both teams masterfully executing strong serves, wicked spikes, and diving saves. The surges and retreats of these remarkable young athletes were nothing short of awe-inspiring. My team was playing like they were on a mission---and, of course, they were.

Our boys' cheerblock remained on their feet. They screamed and bounced up and down every time we scored. We raced to a 12-8 lead. Only three more points! Shelley was seated next to me and she grabbed my hand in a vicious, sustained grip. Suddenly our team fell apart. We made three errors---two spikes out of bounds and a hand touching the net. Brian then pounded a pair of kills to our floor and all of a sudden Clay owned a 13-12 lead. Clay was only two points from the victory.

I called my final time-out. The clock showed only twenty seconds remaining in the game. These were the types of competitive situations in which I had thrived as a basketball player. *Give me the ball,* I'd have said. *Let me take the last shot,* I would have begged. But now as a coach, I felt helpless. The time of reckoning was upon my team. How would they respond?

"Now is when we make history!" I shouted to the girls in our tight huddle. "This is where we dig to our deepest core. Keep the ball away from Brian, and let's end this thing!"

Back on the court, as if they had a sudden infusion of ice in their veins, Liz slammed a hard hit to Clay's back court and Sallie stuffed a Clay spike to their floor. We had battled to a precarious 14-13 lead. With a mere two seconds left on the clock, Kasey set a high ball to Annie who rolled a soft hit toward the net. The ball hit the top of the net and rolled delicately along the top net tape like a bowling ball clinging to its gutter. It seemed to suspend there forever, as one of those rare moments in life when time stands still. The crowd was on its feet, and the players on our bench grasped each other's hands and leaned forward in anticipation. Thousands of pairs of eyes were focused on the white leather sphere rotating along the top of the net. The game, the match, and our season rolled with that ball. Suddenly it dropped serendipitously onto the sideline of Clay's court. A Clay player made a futile dive to reach it, and the referee who had been the thorn in our side at the Carmel regional immediately signaled an emphatic "in." Game over! My team had rallied to win, 15-13!

The players on our bench exploded from their seats and mobbed their jubilant teammates on the floor. The team became a human mound on the floor, with arms hugging and tears flowing. Susie, our manager, grabbed me and squeezed so hard I thought I was going to pass out.

Victory!

I composed myself and walked over to politely shake Coach Joan Mitchell's hand. "Good match," was all that I could squeak out before I turned and sprinted to my team to join in their celebration.

Mr. Lemna and Mr. Carmichael tossed decorum aside and pushed their way through the crowd down to the court from the top of the arena. They ran from girl to girl hugging and beaming. I gathered my team and we marched in a line to shake hands with the Clay players, who were standing dejectedly on the sideline. Their faces were wet with tears, as we congratulated them on a hard-fought match. I could tell Brian was exhausted. He was leaning over, resting his hands on his knees, hardly able to stand.

I patted him on the back. "You played one heck of a match," I said. He simply nodded and attempted a weak smile.

The boys' cheerblock and parents of the girls began flooding the court. I met Jim at the sideline and we embraced. It was only then I began to cry. Tears of joy and relief filled my eyes.

"You did it!" he hollered as he lifted me off the floor in a tight hug. "That was unbelievable!"

Before I could answer, I felt a tug on my leg. The players hoisted me onto their shoulders. As they paraded me around the court I looked up in the bleachers and saw hundreds of women and girls clapping and cheering. *This is for all of you,* I thought as I waved to them. My joy was so overwhelming that I wished I could freeze-frame the moment to taste it everyday the rest of my life.

"Please take your seats for the awarding of the medals," Patricia Roy, the director of girls' athletics for the IHSAA, announced over the loud speaker, interrupting the pandemonium. Ms. Roy was one of two women on the IHSAA executive board. She had been vocal in her opposition to the boys playing on Clay's team, but had had to defer to the commissioner's ruling.

"Let's congratulate the second-place finishers, the South Bend Clay Colonials," Ms. Roy proclaimed. She turned to face the Clay team. "Come forward for your medals."

The Clay team trudged to the middle of the court as Ms. Roy and Sue Parrish, the other woman on the executive board, carried the red-ribboned silver medals to meet them. The spectators applauded politely while the South Bend Clay fans cheered loudly. At that moment seven women spectators rose simultaneously from their seats in the second row of the bleachers and slowly paraded across the court directly in front of the Clay team toward the exit. I recognized these women as members of the IHSAA advisory committee for girls' athletics. Their leader was the woman who had called last week to ask me to attend their protest meeting in Indianapolis. Rather than assisting with the awards ceremony as they normally would, this group chose to silently protest the inclusion of the boys in the girls' tournament by walking out in front of the entire crowd. The murmurs that were moving through the arena turned into rousing applause once everyone comprehended what was happening. Even though I understood the intent of their demonstration, I was disappointed that they were not staying to honor *my* team. Stunned at what I was witnessing, I sat on the team bench alongside my players, waiting our turn to receive our medals. I realized this was an unprecedented, historic event unfolding before my eyes.

As I watched the South Bend Clay players lower their heads for placement of their second-place medals around their necks, I felt a range of emotions. I felt sorry for the girls on their team. They had endured a competition where hostility toward their team negated the positive experience to which they should have been entitled. I even felt a little sorry for Brian and Ed. Playing in a state final should be a joyful experience for every high school athlete. They were all denied this joy. But I swelled with pride for my girls. They exuded everything that was good about sports---striving to reach a goal that at times seemed impossible. They overcame adversity and played selflessly. I also felt pride for the boys in our school who had respected and supported the girls for their athleticism and accomplishments.

"And now let's congratulate the 1975 girls' state volleyball champions, Muncie Northside High School!" Ms. Roy shouted enthusiastically over the loud speaker.

Captains Kasey and Annie led the team to the center of the court to a thundering standing ovation. As the girls pirouetted and waved to every corner of the arena, the boys' cheerblock began singing the school fight song. The fans clapped their hands enthusiastically to the beat. When Pat Roy placed the medal around my neck she whispered in my ear. "This event was one of the most bitter pills I've had to swallow in my entire career. But your team's courageous performance made it easier to get down. It is beyond my comprehension how one male could dominate a contest!"

"Thank you," I responded. "It was no big deal," I quipped. "I've been beating boys my entire life!" She laughed and nodded her head.

As I watched my girls receive their medals, I couldn't help but think that somewhere in this country there was a little girl setting a volleyball, shooting baskets, swinging a softball bat, or kicking a soccer ball with hopes of having a state championship medal draped around her neck someday. Unlike when I was her age, this little girl's hopes and dreams could now become a reality. Separate-but-equal sports programs will continue to evolve so that both boys *and* girls will be able to experience the numerous benefits sports competition provides. This is the way it should be. It is only right. Thankfully, I had found my mission in life. I now wanted the privilege of being that little girl's coach.

1975 Indiana State Champions

EPILOGUE

Law professor and former Olympic swimming gold medalist Nancy Hogshead-Makar contends that Title IX has had a greater effect on women's lives than any other legislation, except for women's suffrage. Most women born before 1955 never had the opportunity to experience the joys of athletic competition. There were a handful of famous women athletes---Wilma Rudolph (track), Mickey Wright (golf), Cathy Rigby (gymnastics), Donna de Varona (swimming), Peggy Fleming (ice skating), and Billie Jean King (tennis). But, for every one of them, there were thousands of girls who sat on the sidelines, their souls hungering for an opportunity to develop their skills and compete. Plus, most of the well-known women athletes participated in individual sports which were considered to be more feminine than the team sports. Even though both the women's professional baseball players who participated in their short-lived league during World War II and the barnstorming All-American Redheads basketball team provided crowd entertainment, neither were viable career options for aspiring young athletic girls. There were also a few random female skiers, boxers, rowers, and surfers who found rare, competitive venues for their sports passions, and there have been occasions when a girl integrated a boys' swim team or Little League baseball team. But these women were the exception, rather than the rule. To have the opportunity to thrive in a sport before Title IX was unattainable for the masses of females. I am constantly amazed when today's young women stare at me in disbelief after I'd say to them, "In my day, girls couldn't play on teams. There were hardly any sports opportunities for girls." Few of these young women had heard of Title IX.

Thank goodness we will never go back to the days when boys played and girls merely watched. Today a little girl can join a soccer, golf, softball, basketball, or volleyball league in most any town. She can play with and compete against other like-minded girls. She can earn an athletic scholarship to play in college. And, more important, she can be a respected athlete without facing sexist comments, social prejudices, or unfounded stereotyping. Social norms have finally changed.

The process of sport builds leaders. In fact, it can transform a person. The challenges, fears, and doubts faced in competition synthesize into self-confidence, determination, and humility. These traits, along with the lessons of loss, goal-setting, and teamwork, carry into the board room, court room, news room, operating room, and science laboratory---venues where women can now excel alongside men. Young girls can aspire to be astronauts, sports reporters, engineers, CEOs, senators, physicians, military generals, television news anchors, architects, and even professional basketball players. They are now exposed to female role models in every facet of life. Witnessing these changes makes me realize I grew up in one world, and am now seeing a better one for women.

*****

In writing this memoir, I have been forced to dig into the deepest recesses of my memory. It is natural for precise details of many life experiences to fade as years pass by. Events and experiences that had been so monumental to me as a little girl and young woman had become lost in the streams of time. The joys of married life, raising children, coaching, and teaching had replaced the desires and hurts of long ago. In my case, however, all it took was the rediscovery of old, stored-away picture albums, yearbooks, and scrapbooks for the memories to ooze into my consciousness. I gazed at photos of my dad and me shooting baskets in the driveway, my brothers and me seated around the dinner table, my classmates from multiple schools and towns, my Indiana University basketball teammates celebrating after a win at the national tournament, the Marion-Kay Peppers boarding a plane for Gallup, New Mexico, and my Northside volleyball players triumphantly lifting their state championship trophies. Yellowed newspaper articles taped in a scrapbook recounted the scores and drama of the 1974 and 1975 volleyball tournament journeys. Newspaper photos showed South Bend Clay's Brian Goralski leaping high above the net. As I looked and read, not only did the recollections become clearer, but I began feeling the emotions that had accompanied each experience. My heart ached as I recalled the tears, joys, and confusion of growing up in a time and place when girls didn't have many sports opportunities, especially in team sports. My pulse raced as I remembered the exciting basketball games in which I competed. My stomach churned as I relived the thrilling volleyball matches in which I coached. Long-lost details even began drifting into my dreams at night---conversations, pre-game speeches, rallying cheers. I could hear the voices and see the faces. Reliving these memories and writing this memoir has helped me appreciate the historic time in which I grew up in regards to women and sports. Looking through my scrapbooks reminded me of the unbelievable accomplishment achieved by my volleyball team at the November 15, 1975 Indiana State Finals, and how that circumstance of playing and *winning* against boys will most likely never happen again at any high school girls' state championship.

My epilogue would not be complete without briefly sharing events that transpired after that historic state final.

- Thanks to changes incurred by Title IX legislation and the expansion of sports opportunities for high school and college women, seven players on my Northside volleyball teams earned athletic scholarships to NCAA Division I universities.
- The Indiana High School Athletic Association (IHSAA) was slow to change their ruling about boys playing on girls' teams. As a result, the year after our monumental 1975 victory, another team with boys on it made it to the Indiana girls' state volleyball tournament. They won easily, annihilating all other teams and finishing the

season undefeated. The IHSAA subsequently sprang into immediate action, and changed the rule. I was amazed it took a state championship *victory* by a girls' team dominated by boys to finally spark the change.

- Soon after winning the 1975 volleyball state championship, the athletic director at Indiana University called to ask me to consider interviewing for their women's volleyball head coaching position. With the upcoming Ball State basketball coaching interview, I was excited and relieved to have two job possibilities for the following year.

- I interviewed for the Ball State basketball coaching position and was offered the job. The result was thirty gratifying years of teaching physical education at Ball State, and coaching women's basketball for five of those years. Motherhood eventually took precedence over the coaching, but I was blessed to earn tenure as an assistant professor of physical education, and retire from Ball State in 2006 with emeritus status.

- Jim and I were married on December 20, 1975, and remain happily married. I can still outshoot him on the basketball court, but he blows me away in road races and marathons. We don't play tennis against each other! He has been a loving husband and a devoted father to our son and daughter, *both* of whom became outstanding athletes and benefited from their participation on organized sports teams.

- Just before the end of my final school year at Northside High School, Mr. Lemna called me to his office to announce that the school board had revoked their rule prohibiting married couples from teaching together in the school system. I politely told him the rule change was too late, and I would be leaving Northside for the coaching position at Ball State University. I could tell he was disappointed to lose me, and I felt sad leaving my teams at Northside, but I was excited to be moving on to new challenges. Jim returned to teach at Northside the following school year and eventually completed a thirty-two-year career as a public school special education teacher.

- Due to declining enrollments, Muncie Northside High School was closed in 1988. It re-opened a year later as a middle school. Our son and daughter attended Northside Middle School, walking the hallways adorned with gigantic photos of their mom's championship teams.

- The new professional women's basketball league (WBL) finally began play in 1978. Approximately 8,000 fans watched Chicago defeat Milwaukee, 92-87, in the first game. There was an all-star game and a post-season championship that year. During the second season, a few new teams were added, while some others ceased operations. Unfortunately, indifferent sportswriters, decreasing attendance, and nervous sponsors contributed to a steady decline in interest and funding. Players eventually endured bouncing paychecks, being stranded at road games, and sleeping on gym floors. They struggled to pay their rents. Travel was challenging, with long overnight trips and players uncomfortably crammed into vans. Meal money became scarce, and several disillusioned players quit. Despite their hardships, many dedicated players continued playing. They didn't want to give up the game they loved. By the third season, financial difficulties became so extreme that one team staged a walkout prior to a game. The league folded in 1981 after three tumultuous seasons. A second professional league was attempted in 1984. It lasted two months. A third attempt in 1986 failed before games were even played. Finally in 1997, with the financial help of the National Basketball Association (NBA), the Women's National Basketball Association (WNBA) was formed and became the first viable professional league. I applaud the players in the fledgling WBL for their pioneering efforts in raising awareness of women's professional basketball. They sacrificed a lot. One player even lost custody of her child when a divorce court judge declared that she traveled too much for her "job." Even though I lamented somewhat about my decision, I was thankful I hadn't given up a secure, tenured teaching position to join the league. I would have ended up short-changed on three years' income, and scrambling to find another comparable teaching and coaching position.

And who knows what it might have done to my marriage!

- As a tribute to their love of the game, four members of the starting five on my 1973 Indiana University women's basketball team became head basketball coaches. Tara VanDerveer garnered the most fame, coaching Stanford University to several Final Four appearances, winning two NCAA championships, and coaching the 1996 USA Women's Olympic Basketball Team to the gold medal in Atlanta. The dream she and I had shared back in college about the future of women's basketball came to fruition, and Tara has become an exemplary contributor to and a celebrity in the sport.

- In 1982, the NCAA replaced the AIAW and began sponsoring the women's college basketball national championships. By this time, athletic scholarships were being awarded to female athletes by most large universities. Unable to compete against bigger programs, small colleges like Immaculata, Wayland Baptist, Stephen Austin, and Lehman were replaced in the national basketball spotlight by well-funded colleges and universities like Tennessee, Connecticut, Stanford, Duke, and Notre Dame. Small schools now have their own divisions and national tournaments. Like men, the Division I NCAA Final Four Tournament for women has a multimillion-dollar television contract and a national audience. With a twinge of envy (and pride), I watch this sophisticated tournament every March and observe in awe the number of *female* sports analysts and commentators who now regularly broadcast this and other women's (and men's) national sports events.

- In 1988, fifteen years after injuring my knee during my senior basketball season, I had my knee evaluated by an orthopedic physician. Even though I had continued jogging, teaching aerobics, playing tennis, and teaching physical education with the same physicality I displayed as a competitive athlete, my knee had never felt quite right. The diagnosis confirmed I had completely torn my anterior cruciate ligament (ACL) that fateful day in 1973. I immediately underwent reconstructive surgery and have been able to continue a very active lifestyle since.

- In 1997, Indiana University invited all female athletes who had competed on its teams prior to 1980 to campus for a recognition banquet. I took my fourteen-year-old daughter to this affair to expose her to a slice of women's sports history. At this banquet we were each presented a letter jacket, the standard award given routinely to all current female athletes. In 2007, I proudly wore my crimson jacket with its distinctive "I" emblazoned on the front to an Indiana University alumni social event in Jacksonville, Florida. Admiring my jacket, every man I met at the function asked me if I'd been a cheerleader at IU. Cheerleading was *still* haunting me!

- In January, 2014, Indiana University invited the women basketball players who played from 1971-1974 to campus for a weekend celebration. We were honored for accumulating the most wins in IU women's basketball history, including being the only IU women's basketball team to advance to a national championship Final Four (1973). We received championship rings and participated in a dramatic Final Four banner-raising ceremony in IU's arena. Forty years after telling Coach Bob Knight how I hoped we'd earn our own banner in Assembly Hall finally came to fruition!

*****

My story is unique…but then again it isn't. My story is only one among the tales of many pioneering women athletes. With this memoir, I am celebrating history. I sincerely hope that today's entitled female athletes appreciate that history, and strive to be positive role models for the next generation. We'll know we've arrived when we routinely hear little boys say, "I want to grow up to be an athlete just like my mommy."

*****

One final story. In 1997, I was sitting in the bleachers watching my daughter play on her high school volleyball team. Entering the gymnasium and taking a seat a few rows in front of me was my former elementary school teacher, Mrs. Edelman, who had vigorously chastised me for playing sports with the boys during recess. Mrs. Edelman's hair was now gray, and her face creased with deep wrinkles. I watched her as she enthusiastically cheered and applauded for her twin granddaughters who were competing alongside my daughter. I descended the bleachers and took a seat next to Mrs. Edelman. She glanced at me and I could see a hint of recognition in her eyes as her mind processed who I was. I leaned toward her and pointed toward the players.

"Times have certainly changed, wouldn't you say?" I whispered in her ear.

She turned her head toward me and smiled meekly as she placed her hand gently on my shoulder. Without speaking, she softly patted my back. We both redirected our gazes toward girls scrambling around the volleyball court and sat in silence.

ABOUT THE AUTHOR

Debbie Powers is assistant professor emerita of physical education at Ball State University. Her lifelong passion has been to promote physical activity and sports participation among girls and women. Her career as a physical education teacher spanned thirty-three years. In the sport of basketball she has been a collegiate player, high school coach, NCAA Division I college coach, referee, and radio commentator. Powers is co-author of ten editions of *A Wellness Way of Life* (McGraw-Hill Publishing Co.). Now retired, she enjoys walking on the beach, teaching exercise classes to retirees, jogging with the Ancient City Road Runners, and traveling. She lives in St. Augustine, Florida with her husband, Jim.

Her website is www.debbiepowersauthor.com.

ACKNOWLEDGEMENTS

My deepest appreciation goes to Bob Furnish for contributing his editing expertise to my manuscript. Not only did he correct my grammar, but he encouraged me to write with extra depth and detail.

Bob Hammel deserves special praise for utilizing his decades of sports writing in correcting my use of apostrophes (*girls'* sports, not *girl's* sports), and other punctuation and spelling oversights. He contributed "eagle-eye" editing on every page, and prodded me to expand my story. Additionally, his enthusiasm for my saga elevated my confidence that someone might actually enjoy reading it.

Thanks also to Eve Stoklosa, Ann Wasson, Kate Powers, Paula Solon, Cheryl Feeney, Kitty Unthank, Vickie Bonanno, and Gayle Krug for reading the manuscript along the way and giving me helpful feedback.

A special thank you goes to Brian Goralski and Patricia Roy for remembering and sharing their honest recollections from the 1975 state championship.

I'm grateful to my wonderful children, Chris and Kate, who encouraged me to write my story, and to my brother, David, for sharing my vision.

Finally, thanks to my husband and life teammate, Jim, for everything.